LITERATURE, THE INDIVIDUAL AND
SOCIETY

LITERATURE, THE INDIVIDUAL AND SOCIETY

Critical essays on the eighteenth and nineteenth centuries

by

Raymond Southall

1977
LAWRENCE AND WISHART
LONDON

ISBN 0 85315 380 9

Printed in Great Britain by
The Camelot Press Ltd, Southampton

Contents

Prologue

This book is based upon lectures delivered at various times and in the normal course of teaching at the Universities of Sheffield and Wollongong. The 'essays' which follow are discrete in that they direct themselves to the works in hand and are not, in my own belief, attempts to trim literature to some comprehensive 'interpretation'. Nevertheless the works considered were not chosen at random and recommended themselves for reasons that were not purely literary. It is necessary to be far more schematic than the 'essays' allow in order to say why the works chosen recommended themselves and how consideration of them extends that concern for the lack of 'any awareness of the communality of human interest' which, at the conclusion of *Literature and the Rise of Capitalism*, I judged to be distinctive of 'the new order of things' in the eighteenth century. That judgement is the starting point of the present book, which thus continues where the former one left off.

In the course of writing *Literature and the Rise of Capitalism* I came to realize more fully than before that once capitalism was established as a social system it created, willy-nilly, its own conditions of consciousness. Its establishment meant the replacement of the old corporate conditions of feudalism by various private conditions; it meant the *establishment* of private ownership and private enterprise, which in turn gave new status to the private individual. It thereby provided the social conditions for the defeat of feudal ideology, as this was entrenched in institutions and propagated by the Church and the Universities, and the basis for the victory of its own ideology, with its focus upon the individual (individual conscience, individual experience).

There is no doubt that, despite the losses necessarily involved, this elevation of the individual made possible a real advance in human consciousness, even though at the same time it contained within itself the seeds of a psychological tragedy. The private individual (unlike the social individual) is doomed to privacy (not sociability) and hence to isolation and a consciousness which sets him over and against society. Eventually he will feel that such a consciousness has carried him beyond ideology and made him an enemy of society's 'attitudes'. This itself is a social attitude and an ideological reflection of the antagonism between individual and society (between individual appropriation and social production) which is a basic material condition of capitalism. Our sense of the individual as private and isolated, then, is part of the ideology of capitalism and just as the imagined relations of servant and lord provided the core of feudal ideology, so those of the individual and society provide the core of our own false consciousness.

With this in view, the present book begins as an attempt to explore the literary consequences in Swift and Smollett of the isolation of the individual, an axiom of modern consciousness having its foundation in the new modes of life established by capitalism in the course of the sixteenth and seventeenth centuries. But the path I chose led me, without any prior determination, to consider the connection between the isolation of the individual and the conditions of life in town and country as these were envisioned in literature – in Gray, Goldsmith and Crabbe – and being transformed by the social movements of the times, specifically by the enclosures. With the recommencement of the enclosures in the mid-eighteenth century it became apparent why, in the imagination, the isolated individual turned from the overpopulated towns and sought refuge in the depopulated countryside. As a social creature, however, the individual in rural isolation realizes in rural life and 'nature' those ideal qualities and relations the absence or denial of which has driven him (at least in imagination) from the towns. These ideals, though comprehensible to criticism, may well be false ones in that they may obfuscate the relations of man to man and of man to nature. This is the case of the pastoral ideals that make themselves felt in the rural poetry of Gray and Goldsmith. On the other hand, as in the case of Wordsworth's poetry, they may be such as to reawaken our sense of human naturalness and community. But Wordsworth's vision of man's place in the scheme of things, I came to realize, needed to be supplemented by one more explicitly and deliberately social, by that of Jane Austen, whose fiction is a sustained attempt to define the ideals of human sociability within the limits of a critical analysis of provincial 'society'.

Finally, in essays on Coleridge and Mill, I considered the romanticism and liberal individualism which did so much to define individual consciousness and sensibility in the nineteenth century and concluded by instancing George Eliot's *Middlemarch* as a novel whose appreciation has been affected by notions of the 'proper' relations of individual and society.

If I had to formulate very briefly what I have learnt in the process of extending my concern for literature's 'awareness of the communality of human interest', I would say that it is that such an awareness is ultimately irrepressible. It may be present as a shudder of horror, as a metaphysical insight or as a belief in the community of minds, but ultimately there can be no lack of such an awareness. What there can be and what there is is difference of consciousness, attitude and realization and this difference can only be understood within the realms of ideology. What the truly great writer achieves is not a vision free of ideological constraint but one which reveals the positive human content present in the ideology which constrains him. The lesser writer merely extrapolates the ideology within which (whether happily or irately) he works.

The Novel and the Isolated Individual

The commanding literary expression of the seventeenth century was the drama. It is equally evident that the commanding literary expression of the nineteenth century was the novel. The eighteenth century witnessed the decline of the one and the rise of the other and it is worth giving some consideration to the reasons for this transition and to the impulses which effected it, if only to question whether it was primarily a consequence of changing taste and fashion and alterations in the entertainment industry.

Like so much sixteenth- and early seventeenth-century literature, art and entertainment, Elizabethan–Jacobean drama was essentially ritualistic. It enacted communal beliefs about man's place in the scheme of things, beliefs rooted in custom and tradition and possessing a religious significance and importance enshrined in the ritualistic nature of the Church, an institution which still dominated every aspect of thought and behaviour. Ritual is the expression of a collective, communal consciousness and in a rite, or ritual performance, the individual is not a representative of, but a realization of something which is neither individual nor personal. We fail to appreciate medieval drama, for instance, when we look upon its characters as personifications or impersonations of one kind or another, where in reality they are ritual figures analogous to those in a tribal dance. Our failure in this is instinctive and is probably due to the decline of collective, communal consciousness in our culture and its replacement by individual consciousness. And if we look for the point in history at which the old consciousness gives way to the new, we find it in the mid-seventeenth century, in what T. S. Eliot misleadingly referred to as 'the dissociation of sensibility' which he dates from this moment. It is a transformation which is evidently reflected, in many intricate and subtle ways, in what is called 'puritanism', that is to say, in the political and religious struggle for individual freedom – not only freedom of individual conscience, but also freedom to pursue one's trade or calling unfettered by ancient

restraints. This individualizing tendency served to atomize the body
politic, it was the tendency of the Reformation and the Renaissance, was
carried forward by Puritanism and had its greatest effect in the
anarchism, the liberalism and the *laissez-faire* of the nineteenth century.
The ideological transformation, the shift in the centres of
consciousness from the public and communal to the private and
individual, indicates the cultural connection between the decline of the
drama and the rise of the novel. Drama, certainly great drama, is
impersonal in manner (there is, for instance, no intrusion of author or
narrator, except occasionally by way of prologue and epilogue) and
public in performance. The novel, on the other hand, is essentially a
private conversation between one individual and another, which takes
place in solitude. In this respect, as a private communication, *Pamela*
would seem to be more perfectly a novel than *Tom Jones*. If, despite this,
Tom Jones strikes us as the better work of narrative prose fiction, this is
because other impulses than those mentioned so far begin to affect the
development of the novel during the course of the eighteenth century.
Richardson's *Pamela* may be looked upon, nevertheless, as a culmination
of the initial impulse which informs the rise of the novel – the tendency
to individualism and to privacy. Just as Puritanism replaced the public
ritual of the Church by private contemplation of the written word, the
Bible, so the public ritual of the Elizabethan theatre was replaced by the
private reading of prose fiction.

The very form of *Pamela* impresses upon the reader the private nature
of the novel's communication, the reader is being allowed, by a fiction,
to read someone else's private correspondence. Even in reading *Tom
Jones* and *Joseph Andrews*, where the privacy of address is partly obscured
by the attempt to provide a comic epic poem in prose, the reader is
constantly reminded that he is in private conversation with the narrator
by those frequent interruptions in which the narrator addresses himself
directly to the individual reader. These private communications, which
the characters are not privileged to participate in nor to overhear, are
those of an acquaintance who interrupts his flow to explain his attitude,
to direct the attention of his listener, to beg for indulgence or to
apologize. They serve to maintain the illusion that the author, through
his narrator, is speaking in private to the individual reader.

Reference has already been made to the privacy of the novel, meaning
that it is an art which has to be appreciated in private, by the solitary
individual quietly perusing the written word, withdrawing from the
hustle and bustle around him to absorb himself in the narrative. That

kind of privacy, it has also been remarked, is intimately connected with the Puritan elevation of the written word of the Bible above the communal observances and traditional rites of the Church. It was in part because of the (originally Protestant) opinion that God spoke directly to the individual through the words of the Bible that so much was done during the Reformation to ensure the spread of literacy. As a result of these efforts, a country which on the eve of the Reformation was largely illiterate had become one which was largely literate by the middle of the seventeenth century. In this very practical way also, Protestantism and later Puritanism prepared the ground for the rise of the novel by creating a literate public, greatly facilitated in this by the introduction of printing and the commercialization of literature. Slowly the mass-readership (or market) for fiction became more significant than the illiterate mass-audience for the theatre and even before 1640 the theatre was providing a more select, indoor entertainment and was on the way to becoming 'the modern theatre', an ingredient in a minority culture, addressing itself to the taste, manners and education of an elite. The increase in literacy and the emergence of a mass-readership, therefore, must also be given due weight in considering the rise of the novel: the reading public had grown considerably during the seventeenth century and, with the quietism which followed the Restoration, the novel was a product well judged to meet a growing demand.

The growth of the reading public had a more particular importance in the development of the novel in that the new readership was largely composed of the new, bourgeois middle-class, whose tastes, attitudes and opinions make themselves felt so powerfully in the work of Defoe and are parodied and ridiculed in the work of Swift. However, the other factors serving to shape the novel, alluded to in the comments on Fielding and Richardson earlier, were the traditional influences of fiction. For instance, the vision of the individual battling against destiny, in one form or another, is quite ancient and is central to Greek epic and tragedy. It is a vision that was somewhat obscured during the Middle Ages, but it emerged clearly again at the Renaissance and is a constant presence in Elizabethan drama, most evident in the tragedies of Shakespeare. The limits which the drama imposes upon the exposition and exploration of this theme are apparent in *Hamlet*: the inner life of the Prince is firmly circumscribed by the need to represent reflection in dramatic utterance, hence, of course, the famous soliloquies. The importance which the inner life of the individual assumed in the course of the seventeenth century could not be accommodated in the drama, even by an increasing use of soliloquy; instead, it found its satisfaction in the novel. The point is an obvious one to anyone who compares a play with a novel and it serves to heighten the appreciation of what the novel is offering.

The scope for the inner life of the private individual which the novel makes available and which could not be accommodated within the drama is strikingly illustrated in Defoe's *Robinson Crusoe*. In many respects, it could be argued, *Robinson Crusoe* is atypical and consequently not a fair example of what the novel initially offered. The reply to that objection is that in so far as it is atypical it is so because it so clearly embodied 'what oft was thought, but ne'er so well expressed': it is unique because it does articulate the ideals of the new middle class as no other single work does. Here, in this one work, is a compelling vindication of the individualism and independency of the God-fearing bourgeois Englishman, already discharging his sacred duty to the Godless black heathen. And to appreciate that this is a new and middle-class vision of the beleaguered individual, it needs only to be compared with that of Bunyan's *Pilgrim's Progress*, which realizes with a far greater power the artisan, nonconformist vision of the heroic individual.

There are other reasons for not considering *Robinson Crusoe* to be something of a freak performance. The circumstances of Defoe's hero could have provided the model for the economic thinking of Adam Smith, for the economic man of *The Wealth of Nations* is an abstract of Defoe's isolated and self-sufficient individual. And stemming directly from Smith, the economic and political liberalism of the nineteenth century grounded its case upon an image of society as consisting of such isolated and self-sufficient entities. If the notions so well expressed by Smith are then traced as they creep across the world they are seen to play their part in the formulation of the American Constitution. In America, as in nineteenth-century England, this image of man produced a body of opinion that believed that each individual had a divine obligation to look after his own without external interference. Rousseau and Blake, Shelley and Godwin, all preached against the imposition of society upon the individual and here too one gathers some impression of the great appeal built into Defoe's isolated and self-sufficient individual. To sharpen that impression it needs only to be considered in the light of that old, traditional view so succinctly expressed by John Donne when he affirmed that 'no man is an island, complete unto himself, everyone is part of the main'.

Robinson Crusoe, then, is something more than a work of fiction; it is the classic expression of the middle-class view. It gives something approaching epic status to that individualism which promoted and shaped the novel. Of a more general importance, however, the vision of life which it embodies informed the consciousness of many generations and moulded the constitutions of states, one of which is still the world's first or second most powerful nation. In the light of such considerations, there is little purpose in contesting the typicality of *Robinson Crusoe*.

What is more to the point is that due weight should be given to the evidence of power which history offers in favour of Defoe's novel.

Robinson Crusoe is by no means a middle-class manifesto; its real quality does not lie in what it claims or suggests but in what it demonstrates. The detailing of Robinson's provisions for life on the island reveals a practical intelligence which gives the hero's self-reliance and independence a real and convincing substance. It has already been remarked that *Robinson Crusoe* is epic-like; its hero achieves epic proportion, or heroic standing, by overcoming the forces of destiny and circumstance, which have divorced him from his kind and left him, an unaccommodated man, marooned upon an island with no more than the wreckage of the life he has known. From the debris and solely with the aid of his own ingenuity and manual skills, he creates a new world. How he does this is the real matter of the novel. The practical problems of everyday life present themselves one by one, and one by one the skills of Robinson overcome them, producing in the process the facilities and equipment of normal life. Indeed, so convincing and finely realized is this narrative performance that the novel seems to present itself as a manual of farming engineering and handicraft. From time to time this practical man's guide is interrupted by pious reflections and resolutions, which become increasingly self-righteous as Robinson sees the error of his earlier ways – and it is this piousness that provides the curriculum of Man Friday's education. So that the characterization of Defoe's hero produces not only an image of bourgeois self-sufficiency and practicality, but also shrouds this in an air of self-righteousness, permeated by a sense of racial superiority. In all, it produces a realistic portrait, warts and all, of middle-class man. It is this which enables the novel to carry such conviction and it is no surprise to discover that, according to legend, many of its original readers (knowing nothing of the story of Alexander Selkirk, upon which it is loosely based) were convinced that it was the journal of an actual castaway.

Several of the works mentioned so far are accounts of a journey; this is true of Bunyan's *Pilgrim's Progress*, Fielding's *Joseph Andrews* and *Tom Jones* and to some extent of Defoe's *Robinson Crusoe*. The common opinion of this device of the journey seems to be that it is a rather primitive framework for a continuous prose narrative, growing out of the much earlier picaresque novels. What the device does, it is said, is to bind together a number of completed episodes, giving the novel itself an episodic character; it might be likened, on this account, to the string upon which beads are threaded in order to produce a necklace. The outcome is what, in the language of the film-maker, would be called a 'series' rather than a 'serial'. According to this view, the serial form of the nineteenth-century novel is more sophisticated.

It is impossible to conceive of *Pilgrim's Progress*, *Gulliver's Travels*, *Rasselas*, *Joseph Andrews* or *Tom Jones* taking any other form. The travel form seems to be organic, to grow out of the substance of the narrative rather than to be imposed upon it for want of something better. More can be said in favour of the device than that, although that is a sufficient justification of it. In *Joseph Andrews*, for instance, the travel form expresses a certain kind of vision and is not merely a contrivance for presenting what Fielding calls 'the history'. The form itself provides the theme of the novel, innocence abroad. Joseph leaves the sophisticated and naughty city, in which his innocence has come under attack, and sets out to return to the rural honesties and simplicities amongst which he grew up. *En route* he meets with many adventures, which provide him with an education in the ways of the world. The process that takes place throughout the novel is one in which innocence matures to virtue through the transformation of ignorance into knowledge, in the course of which transformation Fielding provides a panoramic view of the social condition of his times, of what Balzac calls 'the human comedy'. The perspectives upon life which Fielding opens up are felt to be inherent in the form he uses.

It is Fielding's comic tilting of the social panorama which places him closer to Cervantes and to Ben Jonson than to any other predecessors. In addition, it gives a large measure of seriousness to his attempt to create a comic-epic poem in prose. For unlike Defoe and unlike Richardson (who was one of his constant butts) Fielding is a comic novelist, according to that definition of comedy which Jonson provided when he remarked that the purpose of comedy is

To paint an image of the times
And sport with human follies, not with crimes.

The art of Fielding, so well defined in Jonson's lines, is quite different from that of Defoe and in some respect (in particular those intimated in Jonson's sense of comedy) prefigures that of Jane Austen. For the continuation of those impulses which give shape and direction to the rise of the novel and are epitomized in *Robinson Crusoe* it is necessary to look to Richardson's *Pamela*. What changes the direction of the novel and extends its scope is magnificently realized by Jane Austen but is also evident in Fielding. Although still intent upon the beleaguered individual, set about by the corrupting powers and influences of society at large, Fielding's comic vision gives real substance to the social world and so serves to place the individual back amongst his kind as a social being. To this extent the titles of his novels are misleading, for the novels themselves do not provide a portrait of an individual – Joseph Andrews, Tom Jones – they provide a social comedy in which the individual participates, acting in part as a foil to human folly.

The claim that Fielding's comedy socializes the individual is not intended to depreciate what Defoe and Richardson achieve. The individualism of *Robinson Crusoe* and *Pamela* has a positive value which complements the sociability of Fielding. For the antithesis of that sociability one needs to look elsewhere, to Swift and Smollett, who supply the negatives to Defoe's and Richardson's positives by way of an intenser, pathological view of individualism. As so often in literature, the intensity is an intensity of rejection (as Dr. Leavis has remarked of Swift) and it is dependent upon a fundamental conservatism, which draws its weapons from the past (as Swift draws upon the metaphysicals in *A Tale of A Tub* and Smollett upon Ben Jonson in *Humphry Clinker*). The past also provides a perspective upon the present and offers some understanding of its tendency, a tendency responded to in the destructive power with which the prose of Swift and Smollett moves from negation and rejection to disgust. As it does so it marks, in a premonition of Romanticism, the isolation and the journey into solitude which attends upon the intensification of individual sensibility. It is, then, not in the sociable works of Fielding and Jane Austen, but in the line of prose which evolves from metaphysical argument and speculation towards a diagnosis of the Romantic sensibility and which Swift and Smollett represent, that the foundations of a critique of eighteenth-century bourgeois individualism are most firmly laid.

Gulliver's Travels: Swift and the Enormities of 'Commonsense'

It was George Orwell's belief that Swift had a great dislike for science and only considered it tolerable to the extent that it was reduced to practicality, to what we would call technology, science as it is 'wholly applied to what may be useful in life, to the improvement of Agriculture, and all mechanical Arts'. Those last words are Gulliver's and are quoted by Orwell, who bases his opinion of Swift's view of science upon the attitudes of Gulliver, a somewhat peculiar procedure since the *prima facie* case for saying Gulliver is one of Swift's butts is so strong. From the presentation of the hero of the *Travels*, one can only conclude, contrary to Orwell, that Swift had little sympathy for that narrow-mindedness which is grounded in an overriding concern for the merely practical, businesslike and computable arrangements of life, which finds its intellectual expression in rationalism and is so neatly summarized (by a perversity of literary history) in Wordsworth's.

> I've measured it from side to side
> It's six feet long and four feet wide.

Wordsworth's lines may well be taken as an instance of the kind of 'commonsense' which Orwell imputes to Swift, an 'acceptance of the obvious and contempt for quibbles and abstractions'.

Orwell is only one of the many who have devoted their attention to what Swift wrote 'about' and, more specifically, to the image of man created in his work. Arnold Kettle, for instance, has also asked, 'Is man really the kind of creature Swift has evoked?' It is much more enlightening, however, to avoid the traps laid by the unhistorical question — 'What is man?' — and to consider who was the object of Swift's ridicule and disgust. Who is it Swift writes for, what kind of person does he assume his reader to be and what is his attitude to this reader? It pre-empts the kind of mistake that Orwell makes simply to realize that Swift has much the same reader in view as Defoe and that it is the difference in attitude towards this reader that leads Defoe to epitomize him in Crusoe and Swift to epitomize him in Gulliver. The hypothesized reader is a man whose enormous self-confidence expresses an unreflecting sense of the inherent superiority of the practical way of life he represents, for his are the practical, business-like pieties of the middle-class Englishman of the time. His 'commonsense', an 'acceptance of the obvious and contempt for quibbles and abstractions', rests upon moral enormities to which he is impervious, although they are uneasily sensed in *Robinson Crusoe* and are brutally exposed in *Gulliver's Travels*.

The implicit definition of the imagined reader and the belittling of this new type of commonsensical man connects *A Tale of A Tub* and *Gulliver's Travels* and provides in the process a vital connection between the prose styles of the seventeenth and the eighteenth centuries. Provisionally, the distinction between the two prose styles can be drawn by saying that the *Tale* expresses complexities of thought and attitude which have undergone considerable simplification in the *Travels*. There is a crisp matter-of-factness about the style of the first two books of the *Travels*, according well with a narrator who is a ship's doctor trained in 'Navigation, and other Parts of the Mathematics, useful to those who intend to travel,' and which serves to create the credulity necessary to the satire. A passage can be taken at random to illustrate the point: the opening paragraph of the book, with its *curriculum vitae* of the narrator; the account, often quoted, of Gulliver's arrival in Lilliput; or such a passage as the following, which serves to prepare for Gulliver's arrival.

It would not be proper for some Reasons, to trouble the Reader with the Particulars of our Adventures in those Seas: Let it suffice to inform him, that in our Passage from thence to the *East-Indies*, we were driven by a violent Storm to the North-west of *Van Diemen's* Land. By an Observation, we found ourselves in the Latitude of 30 Degrees 2 Minutes South. Twelve of our Crew were dead by immoderate Labour, and ill Food; the rest were in a very weak Condition.

This is in the style of a competent witness, eschewing imagery and the kind of speculation to which it gives rise and sticking closely to the facts of the matter as these might appear in a ship's log book. We might compare such a passage with one that typifies the style of the *Tale*; a passage chosen with more care to indicate an obvious earlier seventeenth-century parallel. The passage occurs in Section XI.

> Their lodgings were at the two most distant parts of the town from each other; and whenever their occasions or humours called them abroad, they would make choice of the oddest unlikely times, and most uncouth rounds they could invent, that they might be sure to avoid one another; yet, after all this, it was their perpetual fortune to meet. The reason of which is easy enough to apprehend; for, the phrensy and the spleen of both having the same foundation, we may look upon them as two pair of compasses, equally extended, and the fixed foot of each remaining in the same centre, which though moving contrary ways at first, will be sure to encounter somewhere or other in the circumference.

Swift develops the notion of their 'rounds' into the image of the twin compasses, an image which, relying upon the justness of the analogy, offers a speculative (and ridiculous) explanation of a peculiar fact. In the last three stanzas of 'A Valediction Forbidding Mourning', Donne makes a similar use of this image to express the certainty of two lovers coming together again after parting.

> If they be two, they are two so
>   As stiff twin compasses are two,
> Thy soul the fixed foot, makes no show
>   To move, but doth, if th'other do.
>
> And though it in the centre sit,
>   Yet when the other far doth roam,
> It leans, and hearkens after it,
>   And grows erect, as that comes home.
>
> Such wilt thou be to me, who must
>   Like th'other foot, obliquely run;
> Thy firmness draws my circle just,
>   And makes me end, where I begun.

The similar image serves to illustrate a more general and significant similarity. It is to be supposed that Swift had read Donne and that (if this was so) the need to express and to explain how a parting led necessarily to a later encounter precipitated, through the mediation of that word 'rounds' with its suggestion of circles, a recollection (whether conscious or unconscious) of the Donne poem. Whether this was the case or whether Swift hit unaided upon the analogy, however, is not the important consideration. What is to be observed is that both Donne and Swift, confronted with fact, look beyond the fact for a means that will simultaneously express and explain it, they think analogically because ultimately they are intent not upon facts or experiences but upon explanations. In Donne, it must often have been observed, facts of experience consort together not because they have an overt similarity but because they have a covert one and Donne's art is bent upon the discovery and disclosure of their hidden connections.

This habit of mind is clearly not that of the *Travels*. The style of the *Travels* acknowledges a new respect for factuality, which shapes the character of Gulliver, making his reliability dependent upon his matter-of-fact attitude to experience. Such a respect tacitly admits to a suspicion of the more complex and curious habits of mind encountered in the *Tale*. Indeed it is significant that the word *curious*, which had earlier signified 'strange' and 'intricate' and was often commendatory, should come to smack of the fantastic, in the sense of the ridiculous, in the late-seventeenth and eighteenth centuries. It is some evidence of that fear of revolution which ate away at the minds of 'respectable' people, encouraging the growth of mental habits which shut the door upon speculation into the nature of things and matured into the rationalism, empiricism and love of order for which the eighteenth century became famous in the history of philosophy and art

The psychological assumptions of these anti-revolutionary habits of thinking are expounded by Swift in the *Tale*, where he describes mental disturbances as 'the parent of all those mighty revolutions that have happened in empire, philosophy, and in religion'. He explains this by remarking,

the brain in its natural position and state of serenity disposes its owner to pass his life in the common forms, without any thoughts of subduing multitudes to his own power, his reason or his vision; and the more he shapes his understanding by the pattern of human learning, the less he is inclined to form parties after his particular motions, because that instructs him in his private infirmities, as well as in the stubborn ignorance of the people. But when a man's fancy gets astride on his reason; when imagination is at cuffs with the senses; and common understanding, as well as common sense, is kicked out of doors; the first proselyte he makes is himself; and when that is once compassed the difficulty is not so great in bringing over others; a strong delusion always operating from without as vigorously as from within.

As a statement of the assumption upon which a great deal of post-Restoration thinking proceeded this is admirable. It not only establishes why the habit of metaphysical speculation fell under suspicion (it disturbed the mind) but it also reveals the 'revolutionary' nature of Hume's remark that reason is and ought only to be the slave of the passions and the 'revolutionary' character of Romanticism, with its insistence upon the supremacy of fancy and imagination.

The attitudes expressed in the passage undergo a subtly modulated alteration as the passage continues, finally elevating the imagination and placing its revolutions as wonderful ones.

> For cant and vision are to the ear and eye the same that tickling is to the touch. Those entertainments and pleasures we most value in life are such as dupe and play the wag with the senses. For if we take an examination of what is generally understood by happiness, as it has respect either to the understanding or the senses, we shall find all its properties and adjuncts will herd under this short definition, that it is a perpetual possession of being well deceived. And first with relation to the mind or understanding, it is manifest what mighty advantages fiction has over truth; and the reason is just at our elbow, because imagination can build nobler scenes, and produce more wonderful revolutions, than fortune or nature will be at expense to furnish.

The process of argument is similar to that more readily associated with the metaphysical poets; it begins with a commonplace observation and then by unravelling its implications arrives at a quite contrary observation. In this way, common belief is reduced to a foible and the folly (or madness) of the common reader is tacitly demonstrated by the rotation of his opinions. Dr. Leavis, in his essay on the irony of Swift, has dealt with the manner in which this is accomplished in the *Tale*'s 'Digression Concerning the Original, the Use, and Improvement of Madness in a Commonwealth'. The procedure, though less complex, is more interestingly illustrated in Section VI of the *Tale*.

The *Tale* purports to deal with the abuses in religion and learning, as Swift explains in the Apology prefixed to the *Tale*.

The abuses in religion, he proposed to set forth in the allegory of the coats and the three brothers, which was to make up the body of the discourse: those in learning he chose to introduce by way of digressions.

In the allegory of the coats Swift recounts how the coats (Christianity) were left in the will (the Bible) of a father (God) to three sons. Peter (the Pope, hence Catholicism), Jack (Calvin, hence Calvinism) and Martin (Luther, hence Anglicanism). The satire deals most harshly with Peter and Jack and, in consequence, one may be excused for forming the general impression that Martin (i.e. Anglicanism, the Church of which Swift was himself an official) is intended as a model against which the follies of his two brothers are to be judged. The passage from Section VI referred to above occurs at that point in the story where Martin and Jack have broken away from their brother Peter because they have discovered that he has misled them as to the provisions of their father's will, especially the provision regarding the proper care of their coats. In the passage Martin is trying to persuade Jack to take care in purging his coat of its papistical trappings.

> Martin, who at this time happened to be extremely phlegmatic and sedate, begged his brother, of all love, not to damage his coat by any means; for he never would get such another: desired him to consider that it was not their business to form their actions by any reflection upon Peter, but by observing the rules prescribed in their father's will. That he should remember Peter was still their brother, whatever faults or injuries he had committed; and therefore they should by all means avoid such a thought as that of taking measures for good and evil from no other rule than of opposition to him. That it was true, the testament of their good father was very exact in what related to the wearing of their coats; yet it was no less penal and strict in prescribing agreement, and friendship, and affection between them. And therefore, if straining a point were at all dispensible, it would certainly be so rather to the advance of unity than increase of contradiction.

This isn't entirely lacking in irony; 'Martin who *at this time* happened to be extremely phlegmatic and sedate' implies (by way of the phrase italicized) that the views advanced approvingly are those of the Anglicanism of an earlier age and hence not those of contemporary Anglicanism. With that slender, ironic qualification one is moved to embrace the reasonableness of the views which Martin urges upon his brother and to agree with Orwell's claim that the *Tale* 'scarifies the Dissemblers and still more the Catholics while leaving the Established Church alone'. Surely here, one feels, Swift is defining the point of vantage, those positive beliefs from which the satire proceeds, as that of an earlier Anglicanism. As we read on, however, we realize that we have been led into a trap; the trap is sprung in the opening sentence of the paragraph following the passage quoted:

> Martin had still proceeded as gravely as he began, and doubtless would have delivered an admirable lecture of morality, which might have exceedingly contributed to my reader's response both of body and mind, the true ultimate end of ethics; but Jack was already gone a flight-shot beyond his patience.

Immediately the moral reasonableness of Martin is made to appear academic, the beginning of 'an admirable lecture of morality'. From where we are led to view our acquiescence to that reasonableness as conducive to moral complacency, to an ease that is mentally and physically soporific, which (we are informed) is 'the true end of ethics'. It is as though we have been caught out approving of Pope's 'soft dean' –

> To rest, the cushion and soft Dean invite

– only to discover that when we thought we were nodding approval we were actually nodding to sleep.

The initial irony of the first passage has already insinuated that the reasonableness of Martin is a thing of the past and now that reasonableness has been judged academic and complacent. The manner in which Swift offers a point of vantage and then proceeds to undermine it, leaving the reader floundering, having offered as solid what he then reveals to be hollow, expresses the basic preoccupation of the *Tale*. What this preoccupation is may be discovered from the author's preface, from a passage in which the comic fictions disclose a conception that is not comic:

> seamen have a custom, when they meet a whale, to fling him out an empty tub by way of amusement, to divert him from laying violent hands upon the ship. The parable was immediately mythologised; the whale was interpreted to be Hobbes' *Leviathan*, which tosses and plays

with all schemes of religion and government, whereof a great many are hollow, and dry, and empty, and noisy, and wooden, and given to rotation: this is the leviathan, whence the terrible wits of our age are said to borrow their weapons. The ship in danger is easily understood to be its old antitype, the commonwealth. But how to analyse the tub, was a matter of difficulty; when, after long inquiry and debate, the literal meaning was preserved; and it was decreed that, in order to prevent these leviathans from tossing and sporting with the commonwealth, which of itself is too apt to fluctuate, they should be diverted from the game by a *Tale of a Tub*.

Swift, then, is offering to advance various 'schemes of religion and government, whereof a great many are hollow, and dry, and empty, and noisy, and wooden, and given to rotation', as a means of distracting wits from attacking the commonwealth. And we have an instance of this as we are lured to approve the reasonableness and solid worth of Martin's opinions only to be surprised in the discovery that they are hollow, dry and empty. We have been diverted by a tub. The same thing happens in the argument about the imagination and the common forms; there we are lured to presume upon common opinion only to discover that it is being turned upside down, which serves to divert the mind by the rotation of opinion. If, then, the style of the *Tale* is judged a happy one, suitable to the ends in view, it must be noted that it is such a happiness as Swift himself defines in the *Tale* as 'a perpetual possession of being well deceived'. To which it must be added that the happiness of 'a tale of a tub' (i.e. a cock and bull story) is that which the deceiver enjoys at the expense of the deceived.

Deception is more fundamental to the *Tale* than particular examples can reveal. The following passages are from the second section.

The worshippers of this deity had also a system of their belief, which seemed to turn upon the following fundamentals. They held the universe to be a large suit of clothes, which invests* everything; that the earth is invested by the air; the air is invested by the stars; and the stars are invested by the *primum mobile*. Look on this globe of earth, you will find it to be a very complete and fashionable dress. What is that which some call land but a fine coat faced with green? or the sea, but a waistcoat of water-tabby? . . . These postulata being admitted, it will

---

* *invests* here means 'clothes', a meaning perpetuated in our use of the word 'investiture'.

follow in due course of reasoning that those beings, which the world calls improperly suits of clothes, are in reality the most refined species of animals; or, to proceed higher, that they are rational creatures or men. For, is it not manifest that they live, and move, and talk, and perform all other offices of human life? are not beauty, and wit, and mien, and breeding, their inseparable properties?

. . . Others of these professors, though agreeing in the main system, were yet more refined upon certain branches of it; and held that man was an animal compounded of two dresses, the natural and celestial suit, which were the body and soul: that the soul was the outward, and the body the inward clothing; that the latter was *ex traduce*, but the former of daily creation and circumfusion; this last they proved by scripture, because in them we live, and move, and have our being; as likewise by philosophy, because they are all in all, and all in every part. Besides, said they, separate these two and you will find the body to be only a senseless unsavoury carcase: by all which it is manifest that the outward dress must needs be the soul.

Swift then continues to inform the reader that 'To this system of religion were tagged several subaltern doctrines' and goes on to instance these as having to do with the embroidery, gold lace and other embellishments with which the coats are bedecked.

Swift's allegory of Christianity as a coat, therefore, is made to seem ridiculous almost at the outset of the *Tale*. In the above passages the reader is made fully aware of the reversal of common opinion expressed in the allegory of the coats and summarized in the contention 'that the outward dress must needs be the soul'. Christianity so dealt with is translated into a matter of outward appearances; literally a hollow mockery on Swift's part. Once again the reader is being diverted by a tub.

Enough has been said to give substance to the claim that the procedure of the *Tale* reduces whatever it touches upon to a hollow mockery, and that in this Swift's wit is essentially destructive. There is no novelty in urging the destructive character of Swift's prose. Swift, Leavis has remarked, 'is a great English writer', and has added that his 'intensities are intensities of rejection and negation; his poetic juxtapositions are, characteristically, destructive in intention, and when they most seem creative of energy are most successful in spoiling, reducing, and destroying'. Even Leavis, who is not given to biographical excursions, finds it necessary to observe that Swift's writings are 'of such a kind that it is peculiarly difficult to discuss them without shifting the focus of discussion to the kind of man that Swift was'. And in Leavis's conclusion the art and the man become inextricable:

> A great writer – yes; that account still imposes itself as fitting, though his greatness is no matter of moral grandeur or human centrality; our sense of it is merely a sense of great force. And this force, as we feel it, is conditioned by frustration and constriction; the channels of life have been blocked and perverted.

It is true that the frustration mentioned here is that experienced by the reader, but it has too commonly been seen as a characteristic of Swift, like the disgust which Leavis also mentions, to avoid the speculation that the style is the man and that the disgust, frustration, constriction and perversion, are indicative of 'the kind of man Swift was'.

To read *Gulliver's Travels* is to find more than a sufficiency of illustration to bear out the insistence that Swift trades powerfully in disgust and hence in rejection and negation. There is, for instance, the notorious description of the maids of honour in the 'Voyage to Brobdingnag':

> That which gave me the most uneasiness among these Maids of Honour, when my Nurse carried me to visit them, was to see them use me without any Manner of Ceremony, like a Creature who had no sort of Consequence. For, they would strip themselves to the Skin, and put on their Smocks in my Presence, while I was placed on their Toylet directly before their naked Bodies; which, I am sure, to me was very far from being a tempting sight, or from giving me any other Motions than those of Horror and Disgust. Their skins appeared so coarse and uneven, so variously coloured when I saw them near, with a Mole here and there as broad as a Trencher, and Hairs hanging from it thicker than Pack-threads; to say nothing further concerning the rest of their Persons. Neither did they at all scruple while I was by, to discharge what they had drunk, to the Quantity of at least two Hogsheads, in a vessel that held above three Tuns.

That expresses a revulsion which is perhaps even more powerfully present in the final book, just as the incident of the Brobdingnagian monkey, which mistakes Gulliver for one of its own, has its counterpart in the assumption of the final book that Gulliver is a Yahoo. The intensity of Swift's rejection and negation is further illustrated in the second book, in which Gulliver reports that the King of Brobdingnag,

> was perfectly astonished with the historical Account I gave him of our Affairs during the last century; protesting it was only an Heap of Conspiracies, Rebellions, Murders, Massacres, Revolutions, Banishments; the very worst Effects that Avarice, Faction, Hypocrisy, Perfidiousness, Cruelty, Rage, Madness, Hatred, Envy, Lust, Malice, and Ambition could produce.

This so closely echoes Swift's own opinion that it is not difficult to appreciate how discussions of the man became involved in discussions of the art; nor is it difficult to understand that, having identified such opinions as Swiftian, there should be a temptation to assume that the King's concluding remarks are likewise those of Swift:

> I cannot but conclude the Bulk of your Natives, to be the most pernicious Race of little odious Vermin that Nature ever suffered to crawl upon the Surface of the Earth.

We are then prepared to assume that Gulliver has Swift's authority behind him when, in the final book, he refers to the sailors who rescue him as 'the most contemptible creatures I had ever beheld' and, if we ourselves have been lured into misanthropy, to agree with Orwell that 'it is difficult not to feel that in his shrewder moments Gulliver is simply Swift himself'. The *Travels*, on such a view, appear to be centrally concerned with the education of Gulliver, the final book representing his graduation to a proper contempt for the disgusting Yahoos amongst whom he is constrained to pass the remainder of his days.

Once that assumption has been made the theme of the *Travels* appears obvious: it concerns the growth of experience as this enforces a lesson in human worthlessness, the conclusion of which is that man is a degenerate beast, a Yahoo. Then all the aruments can be mustered: man is ridiculed in the form of the pretentious Lilliputians; his social, political and physical life become objects of disgust in the land of Brobdingnag; in Laputa the world of human learning is caricatured and ridiculed; and finally we confront the Yahoo, degenerate man, in the land of the noble horse. In such a way, and with ample quotation, a powerful case can be made out for the misanthropy of the *Travels*. But power is no guarantee of truth and justness of observation and is often the product of simplifications which overlook or discount the subtleties that constitute art.

It is important, for instance, to remark that the misanthropic vision in the *Travels* is that of Gulliver, the narrator, and that the primary judgement involved is therefore a judgement of Gulliver rather than of mankind in general. To ask 'How do we see mankind in *Gulliver's Travels?*' is not to ask a critical question. The critical questions are 'How do we see Gulliver?' and then 'How do we judge his opinions of mankind?' And these are questions of characterization in its fullest sense, as a matter of style, rather than questions to be answered by recounting Gulliver's declared opinions.

There is, as has already been remarked, a matter-of-factness about the early books of the *Travels*, in keeping with the character of the narrator and necessary to the creation of credulity. Initially, the character of Gulliver is of a kind for which the English have been both admired and ridiculed, that of practical, down-to-earth common-sense. The social and political essence of the English character thus seen is its complacency; in place of moral principle it has that patriotic conservatism which accepts the done-thing because it is the done-thing and because it is 'the English way'. Thus Gulliver's account of the state of affairs in England, which he gives to the King of Brobdingnag, is not only felt by Gulliver to be the plain unvarnished truth but, since it is the truth about the done-things in England, it is also felt to be a matter of patriotic pride. It is the King of Brobdingnag who brings moral judgement to bear upon the account when he concludes the interview by remarking to Gulliver,

My little friend Grildrig; you have made a most admirable panegyric upon your country. You have clearly proved that ignorance, idleness, and vice are the proper ingredients for qualifying a legislator. That laws are best explained, interpreted, and applied by those whose interests and abilities lie in perverting, confounding, and eluding them. I observe among you some lines of an institution, which in its original might have been tolerable; but these half erased, and the rest wholly blurred and blotted by corruptions. It doth not appear from all you have said, how any one perfection is required towards the procurement of any one station among you; much less that men are ennobled on account of their virtue, that priests are advanced for their piety or learning, soldiers for their conduct or valour, judges for their integrity, senators for the love of their country, or counsellors for their wisdom. As for yourself (continued the king) who have spent the greatest part of your life travelling; I am well disposed to hope you may hitherto have escaped many vices of your country. But, by what I have gathered from your own relation, and the answers I have with much pains wringed and extorted from you; I cannot but conclude the bulk of your natives, to be the most pernicious race of little odious vermin that nature ever suffered to crawl upon the surface of the Earth.

It is difficult to see how any other judgement of Gulliver's smug and complacent view of his country could have been made. It must be noted, however, that what is involved is a judgement of England as seen by Gulliver and not necessarily of England as it was or as Swift believed it to be. It is important to remark this, for it is the key to the development of the narrator and hence of the narrative.

Perhaps the best way of revealing this development is by simple comparison. In the first book, Reldresal gives Gulliver the following account of Lilliputian religious controversy and of the relations ensuing between 'the two great empires of Lilliput and Blefuscu':

It is computed, that eleven thousands have, at several times, suffered death, rather than submit to break their eggs at the smaller end. Many hundred large volumes have been published upon this controversy: But the books of the Big-Endians have been long forbidden, and the whole party rendered incapable by Law of holding employments. During the course of these troubles, the emperors of Blefuscu did frequently expostulate by their ambassadors, accusing us of making a schism in religion, by offending against a fundamental doctrine of our great prophet Lustrog, in the fifty-fourth chapter of the Brundrecal, (which is their Alcoran). This, however, is thought to be a mere strain upon the text: for the words are these; *That all believers shall break their eggs at the convenient end*: and which is the convenient end, seems, in my humble opinion, to be left to every man's conscience, or at least in the power of the chief magistrate to determine. Now the Big-Endian exiles have found so much credit in the emperor of Blefuscu's court; and so much private assistance and encouragement from their party at home, that a bloody war hath been carried on between the two empires for six and thirty Moons with various success; during which time we have lost forty capital ships, and a much greater number of smaller vessels, together with thirty thousand of our best seamen and soldiers; and the damage received by the enemy is reckoned to be somewhat greater than ours.

The passage to which this might be compared is that of the fourth book, in which Gulliver gives his master, the Houynhnm, an opinion as to the 'causes or motives that made one country go to war with another'. They include, according to Gulliver,

> Sometimes the ambition of princes, who never think they have land or people enough to govern: Sometimes the corruption of ministers, who engage their master in a war in order to stifle or divert the clamour of the subjects against their evil administration. Difference in opinions hath cost many millions of lives: for instance, whether flesh be bread, or bread be flesh: whether the juice of a certain berry be blood or wine: whether whistling be a vice or a virtue: whether it be better to kiss a post, or throw it into the fire: what is the best colour for a coat, whether black, red, white or grey; and whether it should be long or short, narrow or wide, dirty or clean; with many more. Neither are any wars so furious and bloody, or of so long continuance, as those occasioned by difference in opinion, especially if it be in things indifferent.

The first passage is a satiric parody of the controversy between Catholics and Protestants in England and the ensuing conflict between France and England. The comic send-up itself is testimony to Swift's own belief in religious toleration. Gulliver, however, is impervious to the obvious parallels between the religious controversies and wars of Lilliput and those of England. He accepts Reldresal's account without comment, as a simple statement of fact. He gives similar accounts of the affairs of his own country to the King of Brobdingnag in the second book, accounts which Swift renders even more outrageous by having Gulliver declare that

> I have always born that laudable partiality to my own country, which Dionysius Halicarnassensis with so much justice recommends to an historian. I would hide the frailties and deformities of my political mother, and place her virtues and beauties in the most advantageous light. This was my sincere endeavour in those many discourses I had with that mighty monarch, although it unfortunately failed of success.

In the third book, after conjuring up 'all the persons of greatest name in the courts of princes for an hundred years past' and questioning them, Gulliver declares himself 'disgusted with modern history'. This disgust marks the account of the causes and motives of war he gives to his master, the Houyhnhnm, in the fourth and final book of the *Travels*.

In such passages, the nature of the narrator's and hence the narrative's development is quite clear: not only is Gulliver's complacency being stripped aside as the work progresses, but it is being stripped aside in order to reveal the repulsiveness of the view upon which it has been founded from the outset. Once Gulliver's complacency has been pared away there is no longer any need for a King of Brobdingnag to expose Gulliver's vision for what it is. What we confront in the *Travels*, then, is this continuous exposure of the enormities upon which patriotic English smugness reclines and what we have demonstrated are the processes of self-realization by which that smugness blossoms into misanthropy.

Many readers, however, feel that in the last two books of the *Travels* the authorial and the narrative points of view merge and that Gulliver becomes a mouthpiece for Swift. It is felt that, although the final books continue the parodies of humanity and of human behaviour, Gulliver ceases to be the butt of Swift's satire as he becomes increasingly repelled by the degeneracy of mankind. The feeling seems to be that in the final two books Gulliver has learnt his lesson and having done so receives Swift's seal of approval. On this view, the structure of *Gulliver's Travels* is somewhat similar to the General Prologue of the *Canterbury Tales* and *Absalom and Architophel*: moving from irony to satire and from satire to explicit condemnation.

What is wrong with this point of view is that it discounts that kind of response which leads us to say that the final two books continue to *parody* humanity and human behaviour; it implies that description replaces parody. This is plainly not so. Indeed the third book contains the most brilliantly comic parodies of the *Travels*, instanced in the description of the works of the various projectors:

The first man I saw was of a meagre aspect, with sooty hands and face, his hair and beard long, ragged and singed in several places. His clothes, shirt, and skin were all of the same colour. He had been eight years upon a project for extracting sunbeams out of cucumbers, which were to be put into vials hermetically sealed, and let out to warm the air in raw inclement summers. He told me, he did not doubt in eight years more, that he should be able to supply Governors' gardens with sunshine at a reasonable rate; but he complained that his stock was low, and intreated me to give him something as an encouragement to ingenuity, especially since this had been a very dear season for cucumbers.

It is worth pausing to remark that Orwell's belief that Swift found science tolerable only to the extent that it was reduced to practicality takes a hard knock from such a passage as this. What the passage very clearly expresses is Swift's amusement at the madcap attempts of the projectors of his own day to reduce science to practicality. The merely commercial-technological approach to science is here represented as a lunacy and, in view of the Swiftian procedures throughout, the representation cannot be discounted as a deliberate *reductio ad absurdum*. However, it seems that those who see the final two books as a statement of Swiftian disgust are in the unenviable position of having to read such passages with a straight face.

But the crux of the matter is, of course, Gulliver's attitude towards the Yahoos, those filthy and libidinous ape-like creatures in which Gulliver comes to see the image of degenerate mankind. His initial reaction to the Yahoos is that

Upon the whole, I never beheld in all my travels so disagreeable an animal, or one against which I naturally conceived so strong an antipathy.

He is greatly disconcerted when the Master Houyhnhnm places him beside a Yahoo for comparison:

My horror and astonishment are not to be described, when I observed, in this abominable animal, a perfect human figure; the face of it indeed was flat and broad, the nose depressed, the lips large, and the mouth wide: But these differences are common to all savage nations, where the lineaments of the countenance are distorted by the natives suffering their infants to lie grovelling on the earth, or by carrying them on their backs, nuzzling with their face against the mother's shoulders. The fore-feet of the Yahoo differed from my hands in nothing else, but the length of the nails, the coarseness and brownness of the palms, and the hairiness on the backs. There was the same resemblance between our feet, with the same differences, which I know very well, although the horses did not, because of my shoes and stockings; the same in every part of our bodies, except as to hairiness and colour, which I have already described.

Naturally enough, the Houyhnhnms, who know nothing of mankind, assume that Gulliver is a perfected Yahoo, 'a wonderful Yahoo, that could speak like a Houyhnhnms, and seemed in his words and actions to discover some glimmerings of reason'. Gulliver is not at all happy at being thought a Yahoo and protests to his master.

> I expressed my uneasiness at his giving me so often the appellation of Yahoo, an odious animal, for which I had so utter an hatred and contempt. I begged he would forbear applying that word to me, and take the same order in his family, and among his friends whom he suffered to see me.

Although his master consents to this, Gulliver henceforth refers to his own species as Yahoos, for, as he remarks,

> As I ought to have understood human nature much better than I supposed it possible for my master to do, so it was easy to apply the character he gave of the Yahoos to myself and my countrymen . . .

And, indeed, according to his master,

> the first two Yahoos said to be first seen among them, had been driven thither over the sea; that coming to land, and being forsaken by their companions, they retired to the mountains, and degenerating by degrees, became in process of time, much more savage than those of their own species in the country from whence these two originals came.

The culmination of this association between man and the Yahoo is to be found in Gulliver's feelings of revulsion and disgust at the common humanity of the sailors who rescue him from his canoe and at the wife and family who meet him with joy and affection. There is hardly anything more comic in the whole of the *Travels* than the account of Gulliver escaping from his family to seek the company of the horses in his stables. It seems even more comic that readers should be impervious to the plot which here, as in the *Tale*, Swift is hatching against them. The butt of Swift's satire in the *Travels*, as in the *Tale*, is the imagined common reader. The reader who urges that Gulliver is finally Swift's mouthpiece does so because he rightly feels that he is being directed to identify with Gulliver. However, the purpose of that direction is to betray the reader to ridicule, to place him at the end as at the beginning of the *Travels* as Gulliver's *alter ego*.

Both the *Tale* and the *Travels*, then, address much the same reader as Defoe does in *Robinson Crusoe*, but whereas Defoe shares and supports the reader's imagined attitudes Swift undermines and rejects them, making them the object of his ridicule. Despite the considerable difference between the *Tale* and the *Travels*, Swift's prose nicely accommodates its destructive spirit to the tendency of the time; the prose of 'metaphysical' speculation and argument giving way to a simpler prose of description and exposition. The change is accomplished by replacing the erudite and scholastic narrator of the *Tale* with the down-to-earth and simple-minded Gulliver, whose attitudes the reader is imagined to share, thereby exposing himself to the ridicule directed surreptitiously at Gulliver. Swift, in short, pours scorn where Defoe heaps praise. What characterizes Gulliver is not practicality but narrow-mindedness, not ingenuity but stupidity, not righteousness but moral enormity, all which characteristics take their toll and reduce Gulliver to cynicism, misanthropy and a peculiar condition of the sensibility, which isolates him from his kind by creating within him a revulsion and disgust at the reek of the human. What is felt to be a temporary excess of individual sensibility in Gulliver, however, becomes a constitutional ailment in Smollett's Matthew Bramble.

The Politics of Sensibility

One of the peculiar attractions Smollett has for the student of English literature is that he lends himself so readily to placing, particularly in *Humphry Clinker*. On the one hand there is Matthew Bramble, whom his nephew describes as 'an odd kind of humorist', a caustic valetudinarian with a kind heart, a mixture from which one can readily believe Jane Austen distilled Mr. Woodhouse, Emma's hypochondriacal father, and Mr. Bennet, Elizabeth's father in *Pride & Prejudice*, a character of 'sarcastic humour', much given to what Smollett calls 'satire'. On the other hand there is the fantastical doctor of the Pump-room at Hot Well, who delivers a Swiftian lecture to Mr. Bramble and the assembly, in which he maintains that the disagreeableness of a stink is mere prejudice:

> for, that every person who pretended to nauseate the smell of another's excretions, snuffed up his own with particular complacency; for the truth of which he appealed to all the ladies and gentlemen then present: he said, the inhabitants of Madrid and Edinburgh found particular satisfaction in breathing their own atmosphere, which was always impregnated with stercoraceous effluvia. that the learned Dr. B———, in his treatise on the four Digestions, explains in what manner the volatile effluvia from the intestines stimulate and promote the operations of the animal economy: he affirmed, the last Grand Duke of Tuscany, of the *Medicis* family, who refined upon sensuality with the spirit of a philosopher, was so delighted with that odour, that he caused the essence of ordure to be extracted, and used it as the most delicious perfume: that he himself (the doctor) when he happened to be low-spirited, or fatigued with business, found immediate relief and uncommon satisfaction from hanging over the stale contents of a close-stool, while his servant stirred it about under his nose; nor was this effect to be wondered at, when we consider that this substance abounds with the self-same volatile salts that are so greedily smelled to by the most delicate invalids, after they have been extracted and sublimed by the chemists.

Those familiar with Swift will be familiar with the style of this particular passage: a fantastical presentation of ludicrous earnestness, in which a hobby horse is bedecked with spurious learning and driven nauseatingly into the mire. The doctor's learning is not merely comic, it is vigorously rejected by both the mind and the sensibilities. Indeed, much of the placing of the doctor's opinions is performed not by the mind at all but by the sensibility, that is to say, by that very prejudice of the senses he sets out to refute. The whole performance is peculiarly Swiftian and transmits with a surprising fidelity what has been called Swift's disgust for humanity in its basic, animal functions. It says something, no doubt, of Smollett's redundance that the passage from which the above quotation is taken is perhaps the finest and most sustained piece of writing in the novel.

Humphry Clinker can be placed, with a certain nicety of concern for the 'words on the page', between Swift and Jane Austen. And that it is so — that one can sense behind the doctor's lecture the discourse on the Aeolians and the schemes of the projectors in *Gulliver's Travels*, as one can anticipate in the characterization of Matthew Bramble the dry humour of Jane Austen — that may well give rise to some uncertainty in the reader's mind as to the stylistic unity of *Humphry Clinker*, an uncertainty which can be formulated in a question. Does the form of the novel, epistles from several persons, excuse a failure to achieve the kind of artistic integrity evident in a homogeneous style?

Before attempting to answer that question it is instructive to consider that uncertainty as to style which arises in the reader's mind when it responds to the recollection of Swift and the anticipation of Jane Austen. That may serve well enough to place *Humphry Clinker* in terms of date, but its critical implications need to be treated with extreme caution. I have no very high opinion of Smollett, but I do have a very high opinion of Jane Austen, and my own view would be that *Humphry Clinker* brings to the attention very clearly the connection between Jane Austen and Swift, which many readers and most critical accounts of Jane Austen fail to perceive. It is true, of course, that her novels do not 'hang over the stale contents of a close-stool' stirring its contents under the reader's nose, as Swift occasionally delighted to do. Her observation, however, upon the education of young women, for instance, has the same acid quality we meet with in what Leavis has defined as 'the irony of Swift', just as the disgust of Swift has its counterpart in what D. W. Harding once referred to as Jane Austen's 'regulated hatred'.

In other words, the uncertainty in the reader's mind as to the homogeneousness of Smollett's style in *Humphry Clinker* may well be the result of a critical fog, which prevents the reader from perceiving what the styles of Jane Austen and Swift have in common. A careful and critical reading of the novel, therefore, may clear this fog and, in doing so, establish the unity of style achieved within its epistolary form. An illustration must for the moment suffice to make the point. It occurs, appropriately, in a letter of that Jane Austen-ish character, Matt. Bramble and has the brevity of Jane Austen's observation upon the education of young women. Writing of Lydia to Dr. Lewis, Bramble observes that 'the girl's parts are not despicable, and her education has not been neglected; that is to say, she can write and spell, and speak French, and play upon the harpsichord'. The irony is pointed up by the difficulty in which Lydia is placed by the arousal of her passions; her predicament underlines the grotesque inadequacy of what passed for the proper education of young women. It is an irony which Swift would have pressed more brutally and Jane Austen etched more acidly, of course, but it associates Jane Austen with Swift and in doing so reveals Smollett's failure to capitalise upon an artistic opportunity. For what distinguishes Smollett here from the two greater writers is that he fails to bring Matt. Bramble's insight to bear upon the predicament of Lydia. In fact, in reading *Humphry Clinker*, it is by no means clear that the author is alive to the inadequacy of a young lady's education and it is by no means sure how we are to take Lydia's own remark upon the coffee-house at Bath, to which

> young girls are not admitted, insomuch as the conversation turns upon politics, scandal, philosophy, and other subjects above our capacity.

Although that doesn't seem to be self-evidently ironic, the presence of scandal amidst politics, philosophy, and other subjects above the capacity of young girls, suggests that the observation is not to be taken entirely at face value. But how then is it to be taken? For it is certainly true that scandal is no more within the capacity of Lydia than are politics and philosophy. My own conclusion is that Smollett is satirizing the intellectual pretensions of coffe-house society by including scandal amongst its intellectual pursuits. In short, he seems impervious to the possibilities for irony which lie between the belief that Lydia's education 'has not been neglected' and the opinion that politics and philosophy are above her capacity. He spots the ludicrousness of 'society's' intellectual pretensions; he does not spot the ludicrousness of its educational pretensions. It is a local instance of a narrower vision and a less profound insight than that provided by Jane Austen.

I mention Jane Austen to make a point by comparison, for although there is an obvious social and geographical conformity between *Humphry Clinker* and the novels of Jane Austen, the sensibility and the perspective of the two authors is entirely different. The artistic core of Smollett's novel (if it may be called a novel) is to be found in the letters of Matt. Bramble and perhaps the best way to characterize this central vision is by means of the other comparison I have been making. Consider, for instance, the following quotation, from the final book of *Gulliver's Travels*.

My wife and Family received me with great Surprize and Joy, because they concluded me certainly dead; but I must freely confess, the Sight of them filled me only with Hatred, Disgust and Contempt; and the more, by reflecting on the near Alliance I had to them . . .

As soon as I entered the House, my Wife took me in her Arms, and kissed me; at which, having not been used to the Touch of that odious animal for so many Years, I fell in a Swoon for almost an Hour. At the Time I am writing, it is five Years since my last Return to *England*: During the first Year I could not endure my Wife or Children in my Presence, the very smell of them was intolerable; much less could I suffer them to eat in the same Room. To this Hour they dare not presume to touch my Bread, or drink out of the same Cup; neither was I able to let one of them take me by the Hand.

This misanthropy, it will be noticed, is grounded in a revulsion of the senses; it is produced in greater physical detail in Gulliver's response to the Ladies of Honour in the 'Voyage to Brobdingnag'. This reliance upon the senses, upon the sensibility, to vindicate an attitude is a device already encountered in the doctor's lecture. On the strength of Swift's partiality for this device, many readers have been led to view Swift himself as a misanthropist, whose disgust for mankind is so intense as to be a physical revulsion. I don't wish to recapitulate the *pros* and *cons* of this view: Gulliver does become such a misanthropist, but that is one of the things which makes him such a ludicrous creature.

We may place beside the passage quoted above from the last book of *Gulliver's Travels*, in which Gulliver swoons at the stench of the human, the account of the incident in which Matt. Bramble, 'half-stifled, in the midst of a noisome crowd', also swoons, recovers and sends for a doctor. The doctor, Matt. Bramble writes to his friend Lewis,

> assured me I needed not to be alarmed, for my swooning was entirely occasioned by an accidental impression of fetid effluvia upon nerves of uncommon sensibility. I know not how other people's are constructed; but one would imagine they must be made of very coarse materials, to stand the shock of such a horrid assault. It was, indeed, *a compound of villainous smells*, in which the most violent stinks, and the most powerful perfumes, contended for the mastery. Imagine to yourself a high exalted essence of mingled odours, arising from putrid gums, imposthumated lungs, sour flatulencies, rank armpits, sweating feet, running sores and issues . . .

Matt. Bramble's proximity to Gulliver in this particular incident, or accident, is evident and well summarized in the report of his nephew, when he writes to his friend Phillips that his uncle declares 'he will sooner visit a house infected with the plague, than trust himself in such a nauseous spital for the future, for he swears the accident was occasioned by the stench of the crowd'.

To both Gulliver and Matthew Bramble, then, the reek of the human proves physically intolerable and both swoon away when exposed to it. In both characters, this olfactory disgust is the consummation of an essentially political attitude – in Gulliver to the corruptness and brutalities of the European power game, in Bramble to the increasing democratization of social life. Bramble's sense of propriety is outraged at the discovery that

> there is no distinction or subordination left – The different departments of life are jumbled together – The hod-carrier, the low mechanic, the tapster, the publican, the shopkeeper, the pettifogger, the citizen, the courtier, *all tread upon the kibes of one another* . . .

The fallacy which occasions Gulliver's misanthropy is not difficult to detect and to formulate – not all men are courtiers, politicians, generals, quacks, mountebanks, and Gulliver is mistaken in believing the part (and that the worst part) to be the whole. It is the ease of this detection that identifies Gulliver for us as a comic butt.

The matter is by no means as simple when we look to the misanthropic humour of Matthew Bramble. It is less easy to detect him in error. That

the old social distinctions were in a state of dissolution was certainly true.
It was likewise true that this was mainly a consequence of a relatively
numerous *nouveaux riches*, who assumed the airs and graces, the life-
style, of the *beau monde*. So that, as Bramble claims, with allowable
exaggeration,

> every trader in any degree of credit, every broker and attorney,
> maintains a couple of footmen, a coachman and postilion. He has his
> town-house, and his country-house, his coach, and his post-chaise. His
> wife and daughters appear in the richest stuffs, bespangled with
> diamonds. They hold assemblies at their own houses: they make
> sumptuous entertainments, and treat with the richest wines of
> Bordeaux, Burgundy and Champagne. . . . The gayest places of
> public entertainment are filled with fashionable figures; which, upon
> inquiry, will be found to be journeymen taylors, serving-men, and
> abigails, disguised like their betters.

Sponsoring Bramble's misanthropy is this feeling that humanity has
'gone to the dogs'. Without the proper distinction between the plebeians
and their betters, the nice and well kept gradations of social rank, mankind had become a mob, a disgusting rabble, actuated (as he puts it) 'by
the demons of profligacy and licentiousness' and 'seen everywhere
rambling, riding, rolling, rushing, jostling, mixing, bouncing, cracking,
and crashing in one vile ferment of stupidity and corruption'. It is such a
scene he sees before him at the ball and it is proximity to it that causes him
to swoon.

Now although Bramble presents a rather exaggerated picture of
society – an exaggeration imposed by his own considerable conservatism
– the picture is essentially correct. It is not, as his reaction tends to
suggest, an entirely new state of social affairs that he depicts, however: it
can be matched, detail by detail, in the social complaints of the
Elizabethans. Nevertheless, one can readily appreciate how the
permanent state of dissolution, introduced into the body politic by the
rise of capitalism and the increasing dominance of the bourgeois upstart,
would lead a traditionalist such as Bramble to a belief that the world had
gone mad and hence to misanthropy.

Here we are in a world different from that of Swift's *Gulliver's Travels*:
Gulliver is an ass, Bramble is not. The serious portent of Bramble's dark
view of humanity may well be lost on a modern reader. We assume,
without any great consideration, that Bramble's horror at the social stew

being concocted all around him is to be put down to mere conservative prejudice. We assume, also without any great consideration, that the social mix which horrifies him is a laudable development in the arrangements of society. In this conclusion we may well be correct. Where a modern reader may go wrong is in the further assumption that since this is so evident to us it must have been equally evident to Smollett and therefore we should not take Bramble's social version too seriously. That, I believe, would be a grave mistake.

Smollett was writing in an age in which conservative views, especially conservative social views, needed to be taken seriously. It was, after all, an age dominated by one of the greatest conservative figures in English literature – Dr. Johnson. The measure of seriousness that needs to be extended to Bramble's opinions of society may be taken by looking no further than Johnson's *Preface to Shakespeare*. One of the weaknesses of Shakespeare, Johnson pointed out, was in his use of dramatic speech, in which he often failed to distinguish sufficiently between the refined and the vulgar. I don't believe that Johnson's point is that in Shakespeare's day the refined and the vulgar were clearly distinguished in their speech and therefore that Shakespeare misrepresents actuality. What he is saying is that a dramatist should distinguish those of high social rank from those of low social rank and that he should do so by observing a certain decorum in his use of dramatic speech.

Johnson's view, therefore, chimes with that of Matt. Bramble: there should be a distinction of social ranks, this distinction should be maintained and any blurring of it is open to censure. Johnson, of course, does not expound this view, he presumes upon it. It plainly appears to Johnson to require no defence, being a view in which all reasonable men of his time would concur. This being so, we cannot dismiss Bramble's view of society as one not expected to meet with general agreement. On the contrary, it seems we must assume that it was likely to be that of most intelligent men of the time.

Bramble's fundamental stance, then, is one which must be taken seriously and in this it is unlike that of Swift's Gulliver. It is, however, a strange, incongruous stance; for although I have concentrated upon his disgust for 'the mob, the herd' (which Flaubert said would always be detestable) this disgust is associated with the considerable warmth, kindness and generosity which Bramble extends to members of 'the mob, the herd'. Just as today it is not uncommon to meet with those who love mankind but can't stand the people around them, so Bramble is a philanthropist when confronted with the individual and a misanthropist when confronted with the mass. The Bramble syndrome is characteristic of what might be called 'the psychology of the ruling class'.

The Bramble syndrome is extremely well managed by Smollett. It consists of a physical revulsion from the 'mob', a chronic ailment which is locked into a detestation of the democratization of social life. An instance of this has already been given. In another of his letters to his friend and physician Lewis, Bramble himself compounds his physical revulsion and his social prejudice, when he writes:

> When I see a man of birth, education, and fortune, put himself on a level with the dregs of the people, mingle with low mechanics, feed with them at the the same board, and drink with them in the same cup, flatter their prejudices, harangue in praise of their virtues, expose [himself] to the belchings of their beer, the fumes of their tobacco, the grossness of their familiarity, and the impertinence of their conversation, I cannot help despising him, as a man guilty of the vilest prostitution, in order to effect a purpose equally selfish and illiberal.

It has been mentioned previously that Bramble provides a fine illustration of 'the psychology of the ruling class', in that he loves the individual but hates the herd. He reveals another trait of that psychology here, confusing egalitarianism with bad hygiene. He is plainly *not* an egalitarian; 'low mechanics' are 'the dregs of the people' and 'a man of birth, education, and fortune' who mixes with them is 'guilty of the vilest prostitution'. His reaction to the thought of eating and drinking with 'low mechanics', even of being in the same room and having contact with them, is that of Gulliver to his family on his final return to England:

> the very smell of them was intolerable; much less could I suffer them to eat in the same Room. To this Hour they dare not presume to touch my Bread, or Drink out of the same Cup; neither was I able to let one of them take me by the Hand.

Gulliver, however, can't stand the contact of his kind because he considers them unhygienic; this consideration is employed by Bramble to strengthen a repugnance for egalitarianism which is basically political, in that it is grounded in the belief that for a man of high social standing to mix with the *hoi polloi* on conditions of familiarity is socially demeaning.

The presumption that the 'lower orders' are unhygienic is an axiom of 'upper class' sensibility and fundamental to what it calls 'refinement': to be 'refined' is to be set aside from the vulgar in matters not simply of taste and manners but also of cleanliness. Such a 'refinement' was becoming increasingly difficult in the later part of the eighteenth century. The towns, and London in particular, were becoming increasingly over-populated as the enclosures emptied the countryside. Bramble is well aware of this, although he fails to understand the cause. He writes to Lewis,

> The tide of luxury has swept all the inhabitants from the open country – The poorest squire, as well as the richest peer, must have his house in town, and make a figure with an extra-ordinary number of domestics. The plough-boys, cow-herds, and lower kinds are debauched and seduced by the appearance and discourse of those coxcombs in livery, when they make their summer excursions. They desert their dirt and drudgery, and swarm up to London, in hopes of getting into service, where they can live luxuriously and wear fine clothes, without being obliged to work; for idleness is natural to man – Great numbers of these, being disappointed in their expectation, become thieves and sharpers; and London being an immense wilderness, in which there is neither watch nor ward of any signification, nor any order of police, affords them lurking-places as well as prey.
>
> There are many causes that contribute to the daily increase of this enormous mass; but they may be all resolved into the grand source of luxury and corruption.

Bramble's view is that farming has been given over to the production of *luxuries* for the towns and that such production requires few hands and therefore many people are displaced from the countryside. This was not true. The lands were being enclosed for large-scale farming, the products of which were transported to the cities for sale. The agricultural revolution made many people redundant, dispossessed them and drove them into the towns, where they were to provide the urban proletariat essential to the industrial revolution. It was not the production of luxuries that was responsible for the agricultural revolution but the transformation of farming into a capitalist industry producing for a mass, national market.

Whatever the cause, however, the effect was to over-populate the towns and London in particular. The towns were not equipped to handle the sudden influx from the countryside and urban conditions of life deteriorated. Urban unemployment, bad housing and criminality were alarming; pollution and disease was rampant; the demand for vast quantities of cheap foodstuffs was met by debasement; the water supply was inadequate and the wells were increasingly supplemented by water from the Thames, which was clogged with the sewage and garbage of the metropolis. Bramble had good cause for his complaint that, in London,

If I would drink water, I must quaff the maukish contents of an open aqueduct, exposed to all manner of defilement; or swallow that which comes from the river Thames, impregnated with all the filth of London and Westminster – Human excrement is the least offensive part of the concrete, which is composed of all the drugs, minerals, and poisons, used in mechanics and manufacture, enriched with the putrefying carcasses of beasts and men; and mixed with the scourings of all the wash-rubs, kennels, and common sewers, within the bills of mortality.

Pollution isn't, as is commonly supposed, a peculiarly twentieth-century problem and although Bramble is given to exaggeration, there is little of exaggeration in his description of conditions in London during the second half of the eighteenth century. Bramble's revulsion at the spectacle of city life, therefore, is not without some foundations in the realities of city life. He may well be prejudiced in his detestation of the mob, jostling together in the city without too much consideration for the social proprieties of rank and fortune, but this prejudice is made persuasive by being stated in terms of physical revulsion. I mentioned earlier the debasement of food in the metropolis, and the reader is persuaded to share Bramble's revulsion when reading his description of the manufacture and sale of milk in London:

the milk itself should not pass unanalysed, the produce of faded cabbage leaves and sour draff, lowered with hot water, frothed with bruised snails, carried through the streets in open pails, exposed to foul rinsings, discharged from doors and windows, spittle, snot, and tobacco-quids from foot passengers, over-flowings from mud carts, spatterings from coach wheels, dirt and trash chucked into it by roguish boys for the joke's sake, the spewings of infants, who have slabbered in the tin-measure, which is thrown back in that condition among the milk, for the benefit of the next customer; and, finally, the vermin that drops from the rags of the nasty drab that vends this precious mixture, under the respectable denomination of milk-maid.

It seems natural, does it not, to be repelled by the physical nastiness of life in the crowded metropolis? By associating that nastiness with the teeming mass of the urban populace, Bramble provides considerable substance for his definition of the 'dregs of the people', for his insistence that anyone who comes into contact with them is likely to be defiled, and hence for his strictures upon those who ignore the distinctions of social rank and subject themselves to the indignities of contact with the *hoi polloi*.

The political attitude and the psychological condition of Matthew Bramble, therefore, do have some considerable foundation in the social realities of the time. One can well appreciate that the conditions of life in London accentuated the values of privacy and solitude and that the demands of sensibility pointed away from the filth and stench of the towns. It is not, therefore, surprising that, as the countryside became increasingly depopulated and the towns became increasingly over-crowded, the urban ideals of Augustan England gave way to new ideals, which centred upon rural life and rustic solitude.

There is an evident connection in the literature of the eighteenth century between the isolated individualism instanced in *Robinson Crusoe*, the cult of sensibility instanced in the sentimental comedy of Steele, and the elevation of romantic, rural solitude, eventually associated with the poets of the Romantic Revival. The connection is one that can be perceived in the character of Matt. Bramble. His beloved rural solitude is essentially that of Wordsworth; it has a moral value which distinguishes it from the commonplace view of rural solitude in the eighteenth century. This latter is well represented in the description of Hot Well which Lydia provides for her friend Letty:

We set out for Bath to-morrow [Lydia writes to Letty], and I am almost sorry for it; as I begin to be in love with solitude, and this is a charming romantic place. The air is so pure; the Downs are so agreeable; the furz in full blossom; the ground enamelled with daisies, and primroses, and cowslips; all the trees bursting into leaves, and the hedges already clothed with their venal livery; the mountains covered with flocks of sheep and tender bleating wanton lambkins playing, frisking, and skipping from side to side; the groves resound with the

notes of the blackbird, thrush, and linnet; and all night long sweet
Philomel pours forth her ravishingly delightful song.

Lydia recommends the countryside as a cultivated city-dweller of her
time might have done. It is a place of resort, 'a charming romantic place',
rose-tinted by literary association. Her references to 'the ground
enamelled with daisies', the 'venal livery' of the hedges and to 'sweet
Philomel [pouring] forth her ravishingly delightful song' belong to the
world of pastoral poetry rather than that of a girl fresh from the Welsh
Marches.

It would be misleading to create the impression that Bramble's vision
of rural life is a novel one. It stretches back through Pope's Moral Essays
'Of the Use of Riches', Marvell's 'Appleton House' to Ben Jonson's 'To
Penshurst'. Indeed, it is well worth comparing Bramble's description of
his life in the country with Jonson's description of Sidney's life at
Penshurst:

> Thy copse, too, nam'd of GAMAGE, thou hast there
>   That never fails to serve thee season'd deere,
> When thou would'st feast, or exercise thy friends.
>   The lower land, that to the river bends,
> Thy sheepe, thy bullocks, kine, and calves doe feed:
>   The middle grounds thy mares, and horses breed.
> Each banke doth yeeld thee conies; and the tops
>   Fertile of wood, ASHORE, and SYDNEY'S copse,
> To crowne thy open table, doth provide
>   The purpled pheasant, with the speckled side:
> The painted partrich lyes in every field,
>   And, for thy messe, is willing to be kill'd.
> And if the high swolne *Medway* faile thy dishe.
>   Thou has thy ponds, that pay thee tribute fish,
> Fat, aged carps, that runne into thy net.
>   And pikes, now weary their owne kinde to eat,
> As loth, the second draught or cast to stay,
>   Officiously, at first, themselves betray.
> Bright eeles, that emulate them, and leape on land,
>   Before the fisher, or into his hand.
> Thou hath thy orchard fruit, thy garden flowers,
>   Fresh as the ayre, and new as are the houres.
> The early cherry, with the later plum,

    Fig, grape, and quince, each in his time doth come;
The blushing apricot, and woolly peach,
    Hang on thy walls, that every child may reach.
And though thy walls be of the countrey stone,
    They are rear'd with no mans ruine, no mans grone,
There's none, that dwell about them, wish them downe;
    But all come in, the farmer, and the clowne:
And no one empty-handed, to salute
    Thy lord, and lady, though they have no sute.

To make the comparison, those lines from Ben Jonson need to be placed
beside a passage from one of Matt. Bramble's letters to his friend Lewis,
in which he describes his life on his country estate at Brambleton Hall.

    Shall I state the difference between my town grievances, and my
country comforts? At Brambleton-hall, I have elbow-room within
doors, and breathe a clear, elastic, salutary air — I enjoy refreshing
sleep, which is never disturbed by horrid noise, nor interrupted, but in
a-morning, by the sweet twitter of the martlet at my window — I drink
the virgin lymph, pure and chrystalline as it gushes from the rock, or
the sparkling beveridge, home-brewed from malt of my own making;
or I indulge with cyder, which my own orchard affords; or with claret
of the best growth, imported for my own use, by a correspondent on
whose integrity I can depend; my bread is sweet and nourishing, made
from my own wheat, ground in my own mill, and baked in my own
oven; my table is, in a great measure, furnished from my own ground;
my five-year old mutton, fed on the fragrant herbage of the
mountains, that might vie with venison in juice and flavour; my
delicious veal, fattened with nothing but the mother's milk, that fills
the dish with gravy; my poultry from the barn-door, that never knew
confinement, but when they were at roost; my rabbits panting from
the warren; my game fresh from the moors; my trout and salmon
struggling from the stream; oysters from their native banks; and
herrings, with other sea fish, I can eat in four hours after they are taken
— My sallads, roots, and pot-herbs, my own garden yields in plenty
and perfection; the produce of the natural soil, prepared by moderate
cultivation. The same soil affords all the different fruits which England
may call her own, so that my dessert is every day fresh-gathered from
the tree; my dairy flows with nectarious tides of milk and cream, from
whence we derive abundance of excellent butter, curds, and cheese;

and the refuse fattens my pigs, that are destined for hams and bacon – I go to bed betimes, and rise with the sun – I make shift to pass the hours without weariness or regret, and am not destitute of amusements within doors, when the weather will not permit me to go abroad – I read, and chat, and play at billiards, cards or back-gammon – Without doors, I superintend my farm, and execute plans of improvements, the effects of which I enjoy with unspeakable delight – Nor do I take less pleasure in seeing my tenants thrive under my auspices, and the poor live comfortably by the employment which I provide.

There is a striking conformity in the vision of country life which these quotations exemplify. They represent a traditional notion of the virtues of rusticity which is by no means despicable and persists in our own day, exemplified in many rural retreats to which the young have retired from the rat-race in an attempt to scratch a healthy, peaceful and unpolluted existence from the soil. There is, of course, a difference between then and now; Bramble, like Pope and Ben Jonson, extols a mode of existence which was traditional and, though under threat in Smollett's day, was still fairly vital.

As one reads through *Humphry Clinker*, then, one does grow into a measure of respect for the viewpoint embodied in Matthew Bramble. To some extent even those social prejudices which are so contrary to our own become comprehensible and take upon themselves some substance from the social conditions of the time. Exposed, as Matt. Bramble exposes us, to the sheer nastiness of urban life, we come (at least imaginatively) to share something of his own enthusiasm for the traditional life of the English countryside. The persuasion of our sympathies this way is, of course, an authorial one. Matt. Bramble, we need to remember, is a fictional creation; the manipulation of our sympathies by the points of view ascribed to him is the work of Smollett.

It may seem unjust to put the matter in this way, to refer to the *persuasion* and the *manipulation* of our sympathies. Those terms might be taken to imply that Smollett has some ulterior motive in the characterization of his central figure. My feeling is that he probably has, although in being ulterior his motive may not necessarily be sinister. But the manipulation I really have in mind is one implicit in any work of art, which must of necessity demand our attention to a partial truth, since a work of art cannot embrace everything and must be selective.

One can conceive a counterpart to Matt. Bramble in the figure of a city-dweller sojourning in the country, outraged by rural ignorance and the lack of civic freedoms. The English countryside, after all, was not stocked in the main by independent yeoman farmers but by peasants and agricultural labourers, working for sixteen hours a day, earning barely enough for their subsistence, ruled by their employer, who was also their landlord and the local justice, and they and their families living in rat-infested hovels, subject to every whim of the local squire. However squalid and unhealthy life may have been in London it was not subject to the kind of feudalism that still commanded the rural areas. One can well imagine a Londoner declaring that he would rather live as a free man in a city sewer than in the fresh country air as a slave.

That side of the total picture of rural life is one that is suppressed in *Humphry Clinker*. In this respect, we might well consider Goldsmith's equally idealizing vision of country life in *The Deserted Village* and compare it with Crabbe's retort in *The Village*. Crabbe answers Goldsmith by a very powerful invocation of the meanness and viciousness of rural life. Crabbe's poem is a grand indictment of those who sentimentalize a life with which they have had little more than an occasional acquaintance.

What is particularly attractive about Ben Jonson's and Matt. Bramble's portraits of life at Penshurst and life at Brambleton Hall is their image of healthy self-sufficiency. In other words, although the way of life they celebrate in these portraits is traditional – that of the self-subsistent feudal estate – this supports the self-sufficient individualism of *Robinson Crusoe*. It is perfectly suitable to the chronic individualism which is characteristic of Bramble. Nevertheless, and as Matt. Bramble himself allows us to see in his complaints at the depopulation of the countryside, the self-sufficient estate and the mode of life it supported was already becoming an anachronism. The estates were increasingly transporting their products to the towns and cities for sale, were becoming increasingly specialized and were themselves purchasing foodstuffs from the town and city markets. The local, self-subsistent farming of earlier generations was rapidly giving way to the farming industry of our own day. The surplus population of the countryside was draining into the towns and the old crofts and small farms in the economically marginal areas (such as the Lake District) were being deserted, unable to compete in town and village market with the new, industrialized farms.

The agricultural revolution of the later eighteenth century was to reduce large areas of the English countryside to a deserted solitude, the inspiration of Goldsmith's *The Deserted Village* and the setting we all imagine when we think of Wordsworth, whose figures, when they appear (usually 'single and alone') are like wraiths haunting the wilderness: the 'solitary reaper', the lone figure of the leech gatherer as he wanders through the empty countryside. Wordsworth, indeed, seems to inhabit the rural solitude that appeals so strongly to Matt. Bramble when he finds himself incarcerated in the city: one anticipates the opening lines of Wordsworth's *Prelude*:

> O! welcome messenger, O! welcome friend!
> A captive greets thee, coming from a house of bondage,
> From yon city walls set free!

And, as one reads on through Wordsworth, the solitude in *Michael, Margaret, The Thorn*, and in so many other of his poems, becomes something sad. There is poignancy in the claim that in this solitude the poet hears 'the still, sad music of humanity'. The formulation suggests some distant sound reduced almost to silence and one detects in it, as in so much of Wordsworth, a melancholia which in reality is loneliness. The compassion one experiences is made more acute by Wordsworth's brave attempt to elevate his loneliness by pursuing what has been called 'the egotistical sublime'.

That, it seems to me, marks the culmination of the cultural drift mentioned earlier; the move from urban sociability (however unhygienic) to rural solitude (however invigorating) terminates in the isolation instanced in Wordsworth and the Romantic cult of the egotistical sublime. It is a long way from Defoe and *Robinson Crusoe*, but it is along the same road. What the figure of Matt. Bramble permits us to see and to appreciate is something of the compulsion which was responsible for that peculiar journey into solitude.

Pastoral Poetry and Rural Life

Although English poetry is hardly to be expected to offer a faithful portrait of rural life, it should be considered very seriously by anyone wishing to understand the peculiar influence this often uncomfortable existence has exercised over the imaginations of civilized Englishmen. By 'the civilized Englishman' I mean one who has his being, either actually or ideally, in the city and not necessarily one who is sophisticated, cultured and refined. Rural life has its own sophistications, culture and refinements and they are in no way necessarily inferior and may in many instance be superior to those of the city. The civilized Englishman may also be one who has his being, again either actually or ideally, in the Court. This type of Englishman, however, ceases to be of any particular importance during the eighteenth century, when, as a consequence of interbreeding, the inhabitants of St. James's became indistinguishable from the inhabitants of the City.

The Court's loss of cultural identity is of some importance in the history of rural poetry, if only because of the closeness of connection between the culture of the Court and the popularity of the pastoral. In pastoral poetry, the sophistication, culture and refinement of rural life are replaced by the civilization of the Court. In large part pastoral poetry represents that impulse to 'get away from it all' which drives contemporary Englishmen into the countryside on weekends. Elizabeth and her courtiers dressed themselves up as shepherds and shepherdesses and spent a day in the fields, enacting the pastoral as do courtiers in Shakespeare's plays. The impulse to 'get away from it all', whether by fleeing into the countryside or dipping into a pastoral, not only provided civilized man with refreshment (a holiday in the fresh air) it also served to distance his cares and anxieties, so enabling him to recuperate from nervous fatigue, and (once free of the normal turmoil of his city life) to recover a sense of perspective, which was morally beneficial. Wordsworth is only one in a long line of poets who mistook these invigorating effects of a holiday for evidence of the special virtues of rural life.

Since the civilization of the Court substitutes for rural life in pastoral poetry, as the Court loses it cultural identity pastoral poetry declines and is replaced by a different kind of poetry of rural life. Thus, at the beginning of the eighteenth century, before the inhabitants of the Court are thoroughly merged with those of the City, we have the pastorals of Pope and Phillips; at the end of the century, when the Court has become indistinct, we have Wordsworth's lyrical ballads.

Although English pastoral poetry is essentially (or at least genetically) courtly in its attitude, it is not uniform in its attitude to rural life. It may attempt to portray real shepherds in a real setting or ideal shepherds in an ideal setting. The difference in aim is important even though the 'realistic' pastoral is no less civil than the idealistic, or classical, one.

The eighteenth century opened with a confrontation between these two versions of the pastoral. In 1708 the pastorals of Pope and Phillips appeared together in Dodsley's Miscellany. Those of Ambrose Phillips are composed on 'realistic' principles and seek to depict English rustics in the English countryside. Pope's are composed on 'classical' principles and depict ideal figures in an ideal world. Addison's journal gave the preference to Phillips, comparing him favourably with Spenser and Milton. Pope replied with a letter which, whilst seeming to enthuse over the productions of his rival, actually reduced them to ridicule and gave the palm to his own.

That Spenser, Milton and Phillips were thought by Addison (and no doubt many of his readers) to offer realistic portraits of English country life suggests, initially, that there was a considerable distance between town and country in the early eighteenth century. Even in London, however, this distance was not a geographic one nor was it due to a refusal to budge from the city: polite society kept and visited its estates in the country. The kind of distance implied is, rather, a special one, similar to that which reveals itself in the charm which country cottages, cottage gardens and village greens still exercise over the minds of city dwellers. The distance involved is that between those who are and those who are not subject to the material conditions of rural life, conditions with which Crabbe was more familiar than Gray and Goldsmith.

The realistic pastoral, however, did not entirely nor yet principally seek to present a vision of the actual conditions of rural life; its 'realistic' principles appealed to decorum rather than to social authenticity. Since the fundamental rule of decorum was that the manner should suit the matter, it was held that the action, sentiments and speech of pastoral poetry should be fittingly 'low' in order to maintain the rustic appearance required by the genre.

Dr. Johnson criticized Shakespeare because the language of his plays often failed to distinguish sufficiently between the refined and the vulgar. This is the criticism which exponents of the realistic pastoral levelled against supporters of the classical pastoral. On the realistic view, the classical pastoral, in being too elevated and refined, failed to express the rustic nature of the genre. On the classical view, the realists failed to distinguish the true pastoral from its later corruption, for although the characters in classical pastoral were rustic, their being so did not carry the implication of 'lowness' for the ancients which it did later. Classical pastoral, on this view, aimed to restore the genre to its original condition, whilst realistic pastoral continued its degradation.

For anyone this late in the day who wishes to take sides in such an argument there are three important considerations that should be borne in mind. The first is that both sides accept the importance of the distinction between high and low and that this distinction is ultimately a social one. It might be argued, of course, that all that this involved was the acceptance of a fact of life: society was divided between the high and low, with a lot of nervous people in-between. Such an argument would be a trifle naïve and does not in any case distinguish between recognition of what is so and the belief that what is so should be so. However, the second consideration which needs to be given weight is that the distinction between high and low was also agreed by both sides to be a cultural one. Now, although it was undoubtedly true that the sociologically 'high' had a culture peculiar to itself and that the sociologically 'low' likewise had a culture peculiar to itself, it was by no means undoubtedly true that the former was a higher culture than the latter. That it was presumed to be so did not make it so and to establish that it was so is an enterprise unlikely to meet with much success.

The third important consideration is one that seems to lend itself more readily to critical inspection. The very use of the terms *high* and *low* carries with it an implication of aspiration and condescension. In this, the realistic pastoral, being guilty of condescending to the 'low', might appear to adopt a stance more likely to lower the value of what it offers than does the aspirations of the classical pastoral. This presumption, however, may prove misleading, since aspiration depends for its merit upon the merit of its goals. It might, that is to say, be judged upon inspection that the aspirations of a classical pastoral are damagingly miscredited. This is the conclusion reached by Crabbe in *The Village* and there is no doubt that on the evidence of Gray's *Elegy* and Goldsmith's *Deserted Village*, the attitudes inculcated by the pastoral, whether 'realistic' or 'classical', distracted the attention and cushioned the sensibility from the realities of rural life.

The Villages of Gray, Goldsmith and Crabbe

Johnson, who later contributed to Crabbe's *The Village*, wrote of Gray's *Elegy* that 'it abounds with images which find a mirror in every mind, and with sentiments to which every bosom returns an echo'. Certain of the poem's sentiments would perhaps have struck a too readily sympathetic chord in the sombre mind of Johnson:

> The boast of heraldry, the pomp of pow'r,
> And all that beauty, all that wealth e'er gave,
> Awaits alike th'inevitable hour.
> The paths of glory lead but to the grave.

The strain is that of *The Vanity of Human Wishes* transposed into a minor key and often closer to gentle melancholia than to the stoic pessimism of Johnson. But that Johnson's judgement of the poem is more than an expression of personal predilection would seem to be evident from the continuing popularity of the poem. The point might be more properly made by saying that it is, or at least used to be, a poem familiar to every schoolchild. In this, however, its popularity is to be distinguished from that which *Pilgrim's Progress* once enjoyed. Bunyan's work found a place in the schools because it was popular, whereas Gray's poem became popular because it found a place in schools.

It is possible that the *Elegy* has failed to appeal to some simply because of its popularity. Dixon and Grierson believed this to be so and argued, with more enthusiasm than logic, that

> The very qualities which have earned for it unbounded admiration have also provoked disdain. But intellectual superiority may be purchased at too high a price, and he must possess a sturdy confidence in his literary judgement who permits it to stand between himself and

the pleasure to which so many minds have borne ardent and emphatic witness.

It would seem that Dixon and Grierson were of the opinion that superior intellect should concede when opposed by 'many minds' and that literary judgement should bow to the principle of the greatest happiness of the greatest number. But to question the pleasure afforded by the *Elegy* is not to lay claim to intellectual superiority nor to oppose 'so many minds', it is simply to affirm the relevance of criticism to an appreciation of the poem and the moods and sentiments which so many have felt to be pleasurable.

It is certainly due to no fault of taste that the most popular lines of Gray's *Elegy* are those of the opening stanzas:

> The Curfew tolls the knell of parting day,
> The lowing herd wind slowly o'er the lea,
> The plowman homeward plods his weary way,
> And leaves the world to darkness and to me.

What is being created here, in ways which have been frequently remarked, is a state of mind in which the careful lethargies of matter and manner produce a mood of quiet reverie. As Pope remarked in *An Essay on Criticism*, open vowels tire, an observation well borne out by Gray's opening stanzas where the effect is deliberate and made explicit in words such as *slowly, plods, weary, droning, drowsy, lull*. The description of the mood as that of a quiet reverie, however, is prompted not simply by the tired movement but also by that slow withdrawal of external interests which 'leaves the world to darkness and to me', 'fades the glimmering landscape on the sight' and shuts off the hearing with 'a solemn stillness'. This whittling down of the senses reduces the full, round tolling of the opening line to the thin and drowsy tinklings of line eight, as the last intrusions upon the somnolent attention are withdrawn to 'lull the distant folds'.

The withdrawal would be total and the journey into solitude complete,

> Save that from yonder ivy-mantled tow'r
> The moping owl does to the moon complain
> Of such, as wand'ring near her secret bow'r,
> Molest her ancient solitary reign.

The exception is as carefully deliberated as the opening mood and movement. The moping owl in the ivy-mantled tower is emblematic; its literal importance is supported by a figurative representation of the persona of the poem, who mopes 'in embattled darkness' (to borrow a phrase from Keats), prizing the solitariness into which he has withdrawn, like an ancient knight who, from his tower, affirms his territorial rights. But the 'ivy-mantled tow'r' and the 'moping owl', figures of the decayed romantic past and of sad, reflective wisdom, also bring into play a gentle melancholy. It is this mood which informs the succeeding stanza, with its elms, yew tree, mould'ring heap and narrow cell. And it is in this mood that the somnolent night-scene of the first four stanzas concludes, with a sleep which has transformed the home towards which the plowman 'plods his weary way' into the 'narrow cell' in which

> for ever laid
> The rude Forefathers of the hamlet sleep.

With masterly care and deliberation the poem establishes its opening mood of reverie shading into melancholy, shuffles off the mortal coil of the senses and by a subtle change of mood and attitude finally establishes its initial somnolence as that of easeful death; the sleep so dramatically presented becomes the sleep of death. The first four stanzas, then, provide the opening movement of the poem in a strict sense, in that they finely adumbrate the range of matter and the essential mood and manner of the poem.

The melancholy of the opening movement is dispelled and the poem momentarily aroused from that sleep which concludes the night scene by 'the breezy call of incense-breathing Morn'. But, like the opening movement, the stanza offers its description of rustic life as a reflection upon death:

> The breezy call of incense-breathing Morn,
> The swallow twitt'ring from the straw-built shed,
> The cock's shrill clarion, or the echoing horn,
> No more shall rouse them from their lowly bed.

And with that final reference to the rude forefathers of the hamlet in 'their lowly bed' sleep once again becomes the sleep of death, the poem enforcing its central preoccupation with continuing elegiac skill. Then the first false note is softly sounded.

So far the elegiac mood, reflective and slightly melancholic, has admirably reflected the brooding attitude of the persona and the tone has consistently maintained this mood. Now the poem turns from its absorption in the mood of the persona to a rather more detached reflection upon rustic life and one immediately detects the first uncertainty of tone and atttitude in the lines

> No children run to lisp their sire's return,
> Or climb his knees the envied kiss to share.

In part it is that *sire* marks a formality which conflicts with the intended display of warm and natural affection. More obviously, however, there is the lapse from sentiment into sentimentality which is detected in the word *lisp*. The uncertainty of tone, then, is primarily felt as a matter of faulty diction and defines the attitude towards the spontaneous affections of childhood sentimentally and the object of those affections as a formal, paternalistic *sire*. This mixture of sentimentality and paternalism is not simply a poetic accident; it becomes a disturbing characteristic of the poetic attitude once that attitude has been deflected from its true subject and the poem turns from the mood of the persona to moralize upon the character of rustic life.

The self-absorbed style of the poem maintains the initial detachment from its rural setting but now too often suggests by this an air of superiority to (rather than withdrawal from) the life upon which it proceeds to reflect:

> Let not Ambition mock their useful toil,
> Their homely joys, and destiny obscure;
> Nor Grandeur hear with a disdainful smile,
> The short and simple annals of the poor.

The *homely joys* and *simple annals* extend the uncertainty of *lisp* and *sire* and are touched with a similar sentimentality and paternalistic care. The detachment here is fundamentally different from the finely controlled withdrawal of the opening movement. It is significant that from this point on the tone of the poem is surest when the matter dealt with is elevated rather than lowly, when attention focuses upon 'The boast of heraldry, the pomp of pow'r . . . The paths of glory', the 'fretted vault', 'The pealing anthem', the 'storied urn and animated bust'. The detached and slightly superior tone finds its most fitting counterpart in allusions to the life of the socially superior, when like speaks to like, albeit in self-depreciation.

A further illustration of the manner in which Gray's attachment makes itself felt as sentimental abstraction is to be found in the use of personification. What this does may be brought home by considering why Gray's reference to Chill Penury could not be an adequate gloss upon the conditions of life which Wyatt outlines in the following:

> The stormy blasts her cave so sore did souse,
> That when the furrows swimmed with the rain
> She must lie cold and wet in sorry plight;
> And worse than that, bare meat there did remain
> To comfort her when she her house had dight,
> Sometime a barley corn, sometime a bean,
> For which she laboured hard both day and night
> In harvest time, whilst she might go and glean;
> And when her store was stroyed with the flood,
> Then welaway! for she undone was clean;
> Then was she fain to take instead of food
> Sleep, if she might, her hunger to beguile.

I am not suggesting, of course, that one should expect anything as Horation or particularist as this from the *Elegy*. The lines are merely offered to provide some perspective upon the life presented in the *Elegy* and only incidentally to suggest that such proximity to the actual conditions of life it views is impossible in the *Elegy*. The poetic mode of Gray ensures that the harsher aspects of rural life are made sufficiently comfortable, and hence conformable, to those for whom the 'high' morality is intended.

The personifications which carry weight are those which bear upon the qualities of that more comfortable life – Ambition, Grandeur, Honour, even Knowledge, although in this last we have to reckon with the transition from the 'polite' to the rustic in the lines

> But Knowledge to their eyes her ample page
> Rich with the spoils of time did ne'er unroll;
> Chill Penury repress'd their noble rage,
> And froze the genial current of the soul.

It is significant that the 'rich spoils' should contrast in this way with *Chill*

Penury, for the contrast serves to place Knowledge as a property of the polite and well-to-do. It reinforces what was earlier remarked about the poem's superiority of attitude, which is present here as condescension. A related condescension makes itself felt in later stanzas:

> Yet ev'n these bones from insult to protect
> Some frail memorial still erected nigh,
> With uncouth rhimes and shapeless sculpture deck'd,
> Implores the passing tribute of a sigh.
>
> Their name, their years, spelt by th'unletter'd muse,
> The place of fame and elegy supply:
> And many a holy text around she strews,
> That teach the rustic moralist to die.

The evaluation which is going on in such turns of phrase as *uncouth rhimes, shapeless sculpture* and *unletter'd muse* is evident, but few readers take the full implication of that reference to 'th'unletter'd muse' which is said to provide the poor man's substitute for an elegy!

It is perhaps natural to the mode of art practised by Gray that its failings should manifest themselves generally as faults of diction; one may refer back to *lisp* and *sire* or look ahead to the final stanza of the poem's main movement –

> On some fond breast the parting soul relies,
> Some pious drops the closing eye requires

– where the word *pious* suggests the kind of forced or artificial sentiment that mars the poem's treatment of the rustic poor throughout. Just as, in the penultimate movement of the poem, the self-reflection of the poet –

> For thee, who mindful of th'unhonour'd Dead
> Dost in these lines their artless tale relate

– is marred by the condescending reference to *their artless tale*. Indeed, the opposition which is felt here between that reference to the poet's lines and that to the artless tale gives local expression to the sense in which the poem's lines invariably suggest a superiority to the rustic life they represent which is a superiority of the 'art' to its matter.

It is in terms of this distinction between 'art' and matter that the inadequacies of the poem's concluding stanzas can best be stated. We can say that the primary matter of the poem up to this point has been the country churchyard and the life which goes on around it; it is this which promotes and anchors the moral reflections. The condescension has been that of the polite and lettered poet looking down paternalistically at his cultural inferiors. In the final stanzas of the poem we are afforded a view of this superior being:

> Oft have we seen him at the peep of dawn
> Brushing with hasty steps the dews away
> To meet the sun upon the upland lawn.
>
> There at the foot of yonder nodding beech
> That wreathes its old fantastic roots so high,
> His listless length at noontide would he stretch,
> And pore upon the brook that babbles by.
>
> Hard by yon wood, now smiling as in scorn,
> Muttering his wayward fancies he would rove,
> Now drooping, woeful wan, like one forelorn,
> Or craz'd with care, or cross'd in hopeless love.

Suddenly the poet-persona assumes the character of a Daphnis or a Lycidas, a figure of pastoral poetry belonging to the world of conventional idylls. The idyllic world, however, is far inferior to that which Gray creates in the opening stanzas and the inferiority is the result of a misplaced sense of art. The poem begins as an achieved work of art, requiring no demonstrations of its own superiority because as a work of art its manner and its matter are one. It slowly becomes a work about art, making assumptions of its own superiority which it finally seeks to substantiate in its description of the poet-persona. The final appeal to poetic fiction is a thin substitute for the real thing, for the poetic accomplishment of the opening movement. And that suggests the sense in which the world reflected in the opening movement is in actuality superior to that of the poet-persona of the rest of the poem. One might sum-up the poem by remarking that it falsely seeks to demonstrate the superiority of 'art' and of what might be called the 'poetic mind'. If it has appealed to so many minds it may have done so by asking them to share its own superior attitude – an invitation it is difficult to resist and which may even give great pleasure, but it is a pleasure purchased by some sacrifice of consciousness.

Although the mood of the *Elegy* at times brings to mind the elegiac pastoral and quietly but steadily insists upon its own superior artfulness, it needs to be borne in mind that the pastoral did have a closer, albeit idealizing, contact with eighteenth-century life than it has with the urban-industrialized life to which we have become accustomed. Until the end of the eighteenth century the foundations of English life were still rural. The mass of the population still lived and worked in the countryside and the ruling class still comprised in some large part the landed aristocracy. Rural life was still assumed to be the nursery of all that was sturdy, honest, forthright and independent and still provided society with stability and continuity and with its sense of fundamentals. What these fundamentals were thought to be is apparent from Goldsmith's *The Deserted Village*, which identifies for us what Goldsmith calls 'the rural virtues':

> Contented toil, and hospitable care,
> And kind connubial tenderness, are there;
> And piety, with wishes placed above,
> And steady loyalty, and faithful love.

In all of which the countryside was commonly (as in Matt. Bramble's case) and traditionally felt to stand over and against the constant innovations, the rootlessness, the moral deprivations and the physical corruptions of the town, at which Goldsmith glances disdainfully in the course of the poem. It is some measure of the changes which took place in the latter part of the eighteenth century that this view of rural life should be a commonplace to Gray and Goldsmith and a metaphysical insight to Wordsworth.

The traditional way of life was destroyed by the class it had so long supported so well. The landed aristocracy and gentry sought to maintain themselves in a money economy by expropriating village lands in a series of private and general enclosures. Parliament, in the latter part of the eighteenth century, was at times little more than a thieves' kitchen in which representatives of the landed interest met together to share out amongst themselves the land of the English peasant and yeoman farmer, reducing the rural population to poverty and driving them from the land, turning so many villages into 'ghost towns' and having a still

uncharted effect upon consciousness and feeling. For instance, Keats'
lines in *Ode on a Grecian Urn* –

> And, little town, thy streets for evermore
> Will silent be; and not a soul to tell
> Why thou art desolate, can e'er return.

– have the large measure of sadness they do, I suspect, because the poet's
feelings about the deserted town flow from a similar source to
Goldsmith's and have their origin nearer home than the poem realizes. It
is against the process that was creating such a desolation that Goldsmith
(a soul who does return to tell why the village is deserted) exclaims,

> Where, then, ah! where, shall poverty reside,
> To 'scape the pressure of contiguous pride?
> If to some common's fenceless limits stray'd,
> He drives his flock to pick the scanty blade,
> Those fenceless fields the sons of wealth divide,
> And e'en the bare-worm common is denied.

The process of expropriation is admirably recorded in the Hammonds'
The Village Labourer. They remark that enclosure 'was often the act of a
big landowner, whose solitary signature was enough to set an enclosure
process in train. Before 1774 it was not even incumbent on this single
individual to let his neighbours know that he was asking Parliament for
leave to redistribute their property.' The landowner's Parliamentary
representative presented the landowner's petition to Parliament and
became by right the Chairman of the Committee set up to consider the
matter, possessing furthermore the power to appoint all other members
of the Committee on whose recommendations Parliament granted the
landowner the right to enclose his smaller neighbour's land. The result
being, as Goldsmith complains, that

> One only master grasps the whole domain,
> And half a village stints thy smiling plain.

Throughout the late eighteenth century, as the Hammonds observe,

> The governing class continued its policy of extinguishing the old
> village life and all the relationships and interests attached to it, with

unsparing and unhesitating hand; and as its policy progressed there were displayed all the consequences predicted by its critics.

What these consequences were are represented by the Hammonds very succinctly:

> In England the aristocracy ... broke the back of the peasant community. . . . The peasant with rights and a status, standing in rags, but standing on his feet, makes way for the labourer with no corporate rights to defend, no corporate power to invoke, no property to cherish, no ambition to pursue, bent beneath the fear of his masters, and the weight of a future without hope.

Uprooted and deprived of a place in English society, the rural dispossessed either emigrated – 'There, far departing, seek a kinder shore,' as Goldsmith puts it – or else they drifted into the towns where they formed an urban proletariat.

The plight of the new proletarian is also remarked by Goldsmith:

> If to the city sped – what waits him there?
> To see profusion that he must not share;
> To see ten thousand baneful arts combin'd
> To pamper luxury and thin mankind;
> To see those joys the sons of pleasure know
> Extorted from his fellow creature's woe.

However, Goldsmith's tendency to sentimentalize the plight of those so roughly and cruelly urbanized is evident a little later in the poem, when he turns his attention upon the fallen woman:

> Ah, turn thine eyes
> Where the poor houseless shiv'ring female lies.
> She once, perhaps, in village plenty bless'd,
> Has wept at tales of innocence distress'd;
> Her modest looks the cottage might adorn,
> Sweet as the primrose peeps beneath the thorn;
> Now lost to all, her friends, her virtue fled,
> Near her betrayer's door she lays her head,
> And, pinch'd with cold, and shrinking from the shower,
> With heavy heart deplores the luckless hour,

When idly first, ambitious of the town,
She left her wheel and robes of country brown.

The passage is respectably pathetic and it is apparent that Goldsmith's idyllic view of rural life is blinding him to the real plight of such young women, which was not that of innocence betrayed and left homeless but of enforced prostitution and such a callousing of the feelings as would have led them to laugh at the notion of 'laying their heads at their betrayer's door'.

The placing of Goldsmith's poem in its historical context is intended to remove the impression that he is guilty of exaggeration. That the effect of the enclosures was not widely known even in Goldsmith's own day (at least not to those placed in sufficient comfort to be included in his readership) is made obvious in the poet's own comment upon *The Deserted Village*. 'It will be objected,' he remarked,

> that the depopulation it deplores is nowhere to be seen, and the disorders it laments are only to be found in the poet's own imagination. To this I can scarcely make any other answer than that I sincerely believe what I have written: that I have taken all possible pains in my country excursions these four or five years past, to be certain of what I allege, and that all my views and inquiries have led me to believe those miseries real which I have attempted to display.

The Deserted Village was published in 1770 and it may strike a twentieth-century reader as rather odd that Goldsmith's readers could have remained for twenty years in blissful ignorance of the effect of the enclosures upon country areas. The historian of Brede, a Sussex village, has written,

> It is probable – as far as the parish of Brede is concerned – that the period of her greatest povery and distress, with its crushing demoralisation, would be during the 100 years between 1750 and 1850.

That the dispossession, great impoverishment and demoralization of the labouring population of the countryside should be unknown to the polite and urban readership of Goldsmith is not all that peculiar, however. It is unlikely, even today, that the situation has improved greatly, if at all, from what it was in the early nineteenth century, when the Rev. G. Alston of St. Philips, Bethnal Green, having described the appalling conditions in which his proletarian parishioners lived, concluded by remarking, 'I believe that before the Bishop of London called attention to this most poverty-stricken parish, people at the West End knew as little of it as of the savages of Australia or the South Seas.' If people at one end of town did not know how those at the other end lived, it is not surprising that they were unaware of conditions in parts of the country still further removed.

What the Hammonds call 'the extinguishing of the old village life and all the relationships and interests attached' to it provides the sound historical fact upon which Goldsmith reflects in *The Deserted Village*. One important quality of this reflection has already been alluded to in the description of the homeless, betrayed female as 'sentimental'. The view of rural life which supports the sentimentality of that passage is expounded at length in the opening section of the poem:

> Sweet Auburn! loveliest village of the plain,
> Where health and plenty cheer'd the labouring swain,
> Where smiling spring its earliest visit paid,
> And parting summer's ling'ring blooms delayed:
> Dear lovely bowers of innocence and ease,
> Seats of my youth, when every sport could please,
> How often have I loiter'd o'er thy green,
> Where humble happiness endear'd each scene;
> How often have I paus'd on every charm,
> The shelter'd cot, the cultivated farm,
> The never-failing brook, the busy mill,
> The decent church that topp'd the neighbouring hill,
> The hawthorn bush with seats beneath the shade,
> For talking age and whisp'ring lovers made;
> How often have I bless'd the coming day,
> When toil remitting lent its turn to play,
> And all the village train, from labour free,
> Led up their sports beneath the spreading tree;
> While many a pastime circled in the shade,
> The young contending as the old survey'd;
> And many a gambol frolick'd o'er the ground,
> And sleights of art and feats of strength went round;
> And still as each repeated pleasure tir'd,
> Succeeding sports the mirthful band inspir'd;
> The dancing pair that simply sought renown,

By holding out to tire each other down;
The swain mistrustless of his smutted face,
While secret laughter titter'd round the place;
The bashful virgin's side-long looks of love,
The matron's glance that would those looks reprove:
These were thy charms, sweet village; sports like these,
With sweet succession, taught e'en toil to please;
These round thy bowers their cheerful influence shed,
These were thy charms – But all these charms are fled.

Compounded in the course of the poem with nostalgia for a lost childhood and youth, such an idyllic pastoralism reflects the longing for a simpler, happier, carefree existence. It calls surreptitiously, therefore, upon feelings of social discontent, but it does so in a regressive and infantile way, by appealing from the real difficulties of the present to the imagined simplicities of the historical or personal past, that is, of a previous age or of childhood. The sympathies called forth by such a vision are consequently profoundly conservative and, like so many expressions of conservatism, have their psychological foundations in the attractions of infancy, hence, the more complex, difficult and demanding the age the deeper and more powerful becomes its conservatism and the more commanding becomes the preoccupation with the child and childhood. Thus, although Goldsmith's lines present a vision with which we may all be expected to sympathize, that expectation should be considered with care lest in fulfilling it we distort our sense of history and of ourselves.

The poem's positive values, its sense of what is right, just, proper and natural, are those of a rural idyll rather than those of rural life. And to a large extent they may be judged to stem from nostalgic mis-representation, a point forced home by Crabbe's poem *The Village*, which places Goldsmith's view of village life as a piece of sentimental hypocrisy and vigorously expounds the dire poverty, brutality and vice, which were common characteristics of the village community.

Historically speaking, neither Goldsmith nor Crabbe see village life steadily and see it whole, but Crabbe's poem is explicit in its bias, deliberately insisting upon the harsher side as if by way of a corrective to Goldsmith's idealizations. Even if Goldsmith's portrait of village life was entirely correct, his appraisal of it would be false, for an idyllic existence may also be an inhuman one. Perhaps the simplest way of explaining this is by quotation from Engels. Like many progressively-minded people,

Engels saw what he took to be the idyllic existence of the peasants and weavers of the countryside being ruthlessly destroyed by capitalist forced collectivization, which expropriated their lands and the communal lands and left them homeless and jobless. But Engels does not see this, as do the Hammonds, as a deplorable tragedy. Why he doesn't appears in the following passage from *The Condition of the Working-Class in England in 1844*:

They regarded their squire, the greatest landholder of the region, as their natural superior; they asked advice of him, laid their small disputes before him for settlement, and gave him all honour, as this patriarchal relation involved. They were 'respectable' people, good husbands and fathers, led moral lives because they had no temptation to be immoral, there being no groggeries or low houses in their vicinity, and because the host, at whose inn they now and then quenched their thirst, was also a respectable man, usually a large tenant farmer who took pride in his good order, good beer, and early hours. They had their children the whole day at home, and brought them up in obedience and the fear of God; the patriarchal relationship remained undisturbed as long as the children were unmarried. The young people grew up in idyllic simplicity and intimacy with their playmates until they married; and even though sexual intercourse before marriage almost unfailingly took place, this happened only when the moral obligation of marriage was recognised on both sides, and a subsequent wedding made everything good. . . . They could rarely read and far more rarely write; went regularly to church, never talked politics, never conspired, never thought, delighted in physical exercises, listened with inherited reverence when the Bible was read, and were, in their unquestioning humility, exceedingly well-disposed towards the 'superior' classes. But intellectually, they were dead; lived only for their petty, private interest, for their looms and gardens, and knew nothing of the mighty movement which, beyond their horizon, was sweeping through mankind. They were comfortable in their silent vegetation, and but for the industrial revolution they would never have emerged from this existence, which, cosily romantic as it was, was nevertheless not worthy of human beings. In truth, they were not human beings; they were merely toiling machines in the service of the few aristocrats who had guided history down to that time. The industrial revolution has simply carried this out to its logical end by making the workers machines pure and simple, taking from them the last trace of independent activity, and so forcing them to think and demand a position worthy of men.

Engels puts the question very nicely: is the idyllic existence, upon which Goldsmith's poem relies for its positive values, a truly human existence, or more to the point, is it 'worthy of men'? The last question is more to the point in that such an existence may be ideal for children, for whom the patriarchal relationship is so important, but baneful in that it imposes upon people a life-long infancy. The inclination to protest that a perpetual infancy is preferable to the life described by Crabbe merely acknowledges the powerful appeal to infantilism which is the surreptitious 'charm' of Goldsmith's view of village life.

There is a further point to be made about Goldsmith's vision of village life, one prompted by the diction in which it is expressed. In reading, for example, the opening passage of the poem, it is difficult to distinguish between the vision which is the result of personal nostalgia for a lost, happy rural childhood and that which is prompted by familiarity with the conventions of pastoral poetry. It seems that the literary conventions are actually giving shape to the personal feelings of nostalgia. In other words, Goldsmith's vision of rural life has been profoundly coloured and shaped by literature and in particular by a literature which owes its charm to its very remoteness from present rural conditions and to its power to conjure up an image of a Golden Age of rustic innocence and simplicity. Crabbe is well aware of this and of its consequences; in *The Village* (and with the aid of Johnson, who supplied the middle paragraph in the passage below) he reminds us that the pastoral is a poetic archaism which does not truthfully represent rural life:

> Fled are those times, when, in harmonious strains,
> The rustic poet praised his native plains;
> No shepherds now, in smooth alternate verse,
> Their country's beauty on their nymphs' rehearse;
> Yet still for these we frame the tender strain,
> Still in our lays fond Corydons complain,
> And shepherd's boys their amorous pains reveal,
> The only pains, alas! they never feel.
>   On Mincio's banks, in Caesar's bounteous reign,
> If Tityrus found the Golden Age again,
> Must sleepy bards the flattering dream prolong,
> Mechanic echoes of the Mantuan song?

> From Truth and Nature shall we widely stray,
> Where Virgil, not where Fancy leads the way?
> Yes, thus the Muses sing of happy swains,
> Because the Muses never knew their pains . . .

But Goldsmith's is more than 'the flattering dream' of pastoral poetry. His poetry reflects in its diction a specially polite and urban sense of fitness, of what is proper: 'the shelter'd cot, the cultivated farm. . . . The decent church.' The adjectives – *sheltered, cultivated, decent* – summarize Goldsmith's own position *vis-à-vis* his chosen subject matter: it is Goldsmith rather than the rustic who is revealed in the language and sentiments of the poem as sheltered, cultivated and decent. His dream of Auburn would readily have accommodated those 'Ranelagh songs' of the day which he describes in *The Vicar of Wakefield* as 'all cast in the same mould: Colin meets Dolly, and they hold a dialogue together; he gives her a fairing to put in her hair, and she presents him with a nosegay; and then they go together to Church, where they give good advice to young nymphs and swains to get married as fast as they can.' To use Engels' terms, his vision of the village is 'respectable' and 'cosily romantic'.

What Goldsmith fails to provide is what Crabbe calls 'the real picture of the poor'. The faulty vision of Goldsmith, as has already been mentioned, is well disagnosed by Crabbe when he refers to the falsification which stems from reliance upon pastoral literary convention, a diagnosis which occupies the second to sixth paragraphs of his poem *The Village*, some part of which has already been quoted above. According to Crabbe, it is necessary to understand the dead weight of the pastoral tradition, reaching back to Virgil, in order to understand the praise heaped by poets upon the rural life, for as he puts it, 'From this chief cause these idle praises spring'. Whilst this is true, it is only a partial truth. The pastoral gives poetic shape to attitudes which find their satisfaction in Virgil's *Eclogues*, but which do not originate in them. Pastoral poetry had its place in the literary culture of polite society because, as has already been intimated, it offered a safe channel for feelings of social discontent which sprang from the deep-seated need for a simpler, happier and more carefree life.

Nevertheless, it may be urged, although poets may have misrepresented the actual conditions of country life, and Crabbe is right to point this out, there was something of real value in it. But let us suppose the rustics' life to be passed in idyllic intercourse with the soil and that they are, in Engels' phrase, 'comfortable in their silent vegetation', yet, as Engels also remarks, intellectually they are dead and know 'nothing of the mighty movement which, beyond their horizon, [is] sweeping through mankind'. Their existence is that of the Brangwen men in the magnificent opening chapter of Lawrence's *The Rainbow* and the inadequacies of such an existence are those sensed by the Brangwen women. It is not intended, or course, to suggest that Goldsmith fails because he cannot match Lawrence's insight, but it is quite evident that Lawrence's power and vision, concentrating upon the Brangwen men and realizing what constitutes the deepest satisfactions of a life spent in intercourse with the soil, is infinitely greater than Gray's or Goldsmith's. The awareness of the Brangwen women is an essential part of that greater power, firmly indicating the narrow limits imposed upon those whose consciousness and sensibilities are of the soil.

It is such a power that is present in Crabbe; it is associated with and perhaps even a function of that closer proximity to the life described which reveals itself in the greater detailing that goes on in *The Village*:

> There the blue bugloss paints the sterile soil:
> Hardy and high, above the slender sheaf,
> The slimy mallow waves her silky leaf;
> O'er the young shoot the charlock throws a shade,
> And clasping tares cling round the sickly blade. . . .
> With mingled tints the rocky coasts abound,
> And a sad splendour vainly shines around.
> So looks the nymph whom wretched arts adorn,
> Betray'd by Man, then left for Man to scorn;
> Whose cheek in vain assumes the mimic rose,
> While her sad eyes the troubled breast disclose;
> Whose outward splendour is but folly's dress,
> Exposing most, when most it gilds distress.

The detailing here is not simply picturesque; it serves to place the human condition which is under review, that of the 'nymph', as part of the natural condition. The description of the 'Rank weeds' which infest the 'rocky coasts' with their paint and silk, their 'sad splendour' that 'vainly shines around', provide a fitting image of the 'nymph' 'whose cheek in vain assumes the mimic rose' (where *vain* has not only the sense of 'unavailing' but also of 'vanity') and 'whose outward splendour is but folly's dress'. Similarly the couplet,

> O'er the young shoot the charlock throws a shade,
> And clasping tares cling round the sickly blade,

is as a metaphor of the 'nymph's' life and character, not only placed
under a shadow by the man who betrayed her, but ensnared by her own
folly.

That last couplet has a further significance, one which makes itself felt
when it is compared with a couplet from the preceding paragraph of the
poem:

> Can poets soothe you, when you pine for bread,
> By winding myrtles round your ruined shed?

The conventionally poetic myrtles, which grace the rural scene in the
pastorals and here wind round the ruined shed, give way in the couplet
previously considered to 'clasping tares' which sap healthy growth.
And this replacement of one image of the countryside by another, the
'winding myrtles' by the 'clasping tares', is the poetic reply to the still
earlier question,

> Then shall I dare these real ills to hide
> In tinsel trappings of poetic pride?

The 'winding myrtles' become local representatives of the 'tinsel
trappings of poetic pride', whilst the 'clasping tares' become
representative of the 'real ills'. But for Crabbe, the 'tinsel trappings' are
themselves one of the 'real ills'; they express a morally obnoxious view
and consequently, in the passage describing the 'rank weeds' of the
'rocky coasts', these 'clasping tares' themselves assume something of the
appearance of 'tinsel trappings', they paint the sterile soil, they flaunt
their silkiness and their 'splendour vainly shines around'. The weeds,
then, express attitudes towards the character of pastoral poetry, the
nature of rural life and that kind of moral corruption at which Hamlet
glances when he describes the world in a metaphor similar to Crabbe's:

> 'tis an unweeded garden
> That grows to seed, things rank and gross in nature
> Possess it merely.

The couplet on the clasping tares is not a particularly prominent or unusual one; it occurs, as has been seen, quite naturally in the course of a passage describing the flora of the coastal regions, a condition to which that of the 'nymph' is then likened – 'so looks the nymph . . .'. But it is distinctive of poetry, when it is working as poetry, that its most straightforward formulations are intimately expressive of the poem's central preoccupations. This is something we are familiar with from our reading of Shakespeare: in *Hamlet* the slenderest allusion to flora is given weight by the extended connotations of Hamlet's reference to the unweeded garden; in *Lear*, allusions to animals reverberate in a similar way, as do allusions to children in *Macbeth*. If, then, special attention has been paid to this one couplet in Crabbe's poem it is not because it is one of outstanding importance but simply because it serves to illustrate the sense in which Crabbe's poem is poetic as Goldsmith's is not.

Goldsmith's poem is too commonly affected by unplaced feelings of nostalgia and the sentimentalities to which they give rise; Crabbe's is very firmly controlled by the judgement in a way Pope would have approved. It is the poetic judgement of Crabbe which ensures the poem's detachment and an impartiality which is well summed up in the following lines.

> Yet why, you ask, these humble crimes relate,
> Why make the Poor as guilty as the Great?
> To show the Great, those mightier sons of pride
> How near in vice the lowest are allied;
> Such are their natures and their passions such,
> But these disguise too little, those too much:
> So shall the man of power and pleasure see
> In his own slave as vile a wretch as he;
> In his luxurious lord the servant find
> His own low pleasures and degenerate mind:
> And each in all the kindred vices trace,
> Of a poor, blind, bewildered, erring race;
> Who, a short time in varied fortune past,
> Die, and are equal in the dust at last.

It is true that ultimately, like Goldsmith –

> Where then, ah! where, shall poverty reside,
> To 'scape the pressure of contiguous pride?

– and his master Pope, Crabbe cannot resist the pull of moral abstraction, and that in his own as in Pope's case, the ultimate tendency is to reduce the complexities of crime and folly to the simplicities of Pride. Nevertheless, he gives a moral status to the poor and the unknown which Gray, prompted by the kindliest paternalism, denies them. In this somewhat perverse manner, Crabbe recognizes the right of 'the lowest' to be treated in a manner 'worthy of men'. To recognize the egalitarianism of wickedness (and presumably of goodness) is not to raise the banners of revolution, but at least it acknowledges that class divisions within society have nothing to do with morality. It stands to Crabbe's credit that he not only felt the enormity of eighteenth-century pastoralism, with its idylls of country life, but also the inadequacy of that more serious, Roman urge to flee the corruption of 'the world' and live off turnips on a Sabine farm.

The Natural World of Wordsworth

Extensions in the range of poetic sensibility, of what is to be generally understood as poetical or as poetically proper, are frequently marked by a deliberate rejection of contemporary canons of taste. One may cite in evidence of this the work of poets such as Donne, Wordsworth and, nearer our own day, T. S. Eliot. The clamour of a new movement in poetry, as in the other arts, tends to direct our attention to a small and articulate *avant-garde* and their figurehead and from there it is only a short step to formulating some kind of Great Man interpretation of literary history similar to that once expounded by Eliot. But as in the case of Donne and of Eliot himself, so also in the case of Wordsworth, the view that a literary tradition lies more or less comatose, awaiting the genius of a major poet to effect a change of sensibility and prod it into new life, does not fit the literary facts.

Wordsworth's poetical radicalism, as it is given voice in the prefaces to *Lyrical Ballads*, points through all its programmatic phrases to the limitations imposed upon the range of poetry by a classical and predominantly urban taste. But well before the publication of the famous preface, these limits were already being extended. Thomson's *Seasons*, for example, are indebted to Milton rather than to Dryden and do not confrom to those standards of propriety of expression which control Pope's *Rape of the Lock* and Johnson's *Vanity of Human Wishes*. In many respects, as recent criticism has made increasingly apparent, *Lyrical Ballads* continue a development within eighteenth-century pastoral poetry – a development one can trace through Gray, Collins, Goldsmith, Crabbe and Blake and which was supported by the growing popularity of older ballad poetry of the kind which Bishop Percy made available.

Whilst continuing and even consummating this development in eighteenth-century poetry, however, Wordsworth and Coleridge appear to have realized that this development was calling into question the old poetic attitudes and habits which still controlled it. In the prefaces of *Lyrical Ballads*, therefore, they clearly and critically point out the limitations of the poetical character of the preceding period and in doing so make the contravention of eighteenth-century poetic precept a critically conscious act. Amongst other and probably more important things, this consciousness of going against the grain of established taste accounts for some of the fervour and hyper-selfconsciousness of so much romantic poetry.

It has been well said that every great poet must create the taste by which he is to be judged and if one was asked to appraise *Lyrical Ballads* as a critical document it is in terms of its attempt to establish such a new taste that it would be necessary to proceed. However, Wordsworth's famous prefaces of 1798, 1800 and 1802 call for a somewhat narrower consideration than this, in particular their strictures upon the poetic practice of the preceding period and their own conception of the origin, nature and purpose of poetry.

Wordsworth, in his strictures upon 'poetic diction', provided a purgative for a poetry which was undoubtedly becoming hide-bound with conventions. The Augustan devices, so magnificently employed by Pope, had petrified; as Cowper very properly remarked, in the later eighteenth century they

> Made poetry a mere mechanic art,
> And every warbler has his tune by heart.

In other words, poetry had almost become a routine, technical exercise in the arrangement of stock materials and the language and modes of Pope had ceased to develop as modes for the expression of lively, felt experience. Against this 'mere mechanic art' Pope himself protested in his own poetic programme, *An Essay on Criticism* (see lines 289 to 382); a point to be borne in mind when considering Wordsworth's appeal against it to fresh experience, to 'the language really used by men' and to first hand observation of men of uncorrupted manners.

Indeed, that last appeal, to first hand observations of men of uncorrupted manners, has often been considered peculiarly Wordsworthian and to constitute a deliberate turning away from the eighteenth century's preoccupation with the *beau monde*. In this, however, he is taking his cue almost directly from Pope. In the second of his essays (189–92), Pope turns from the self-inflated importance of the *beau monde* to the honesty of the lower classes, declaring,

> That robe of quality so struts and swells
> None see what parts of nature it conceals.
> Th' exactest traits of body or of mind
> We owe to models of an humble kind.

Pope here formulates one of the key doctrines of Wordsworth's programme:

> Th' exactest traits of body or of mind
> We owe to models of an humble kind.

His defection from the *beau monde* anticipates that of Wordsworth, who 'turned to models of an humble kind' because, as he explained in the preface to *Lyrical Ballads*, they are 'less under the influence of social vanity'.

This point, the essential continuity between Pope and Wordswoth, needs pressing in order to arrive at a proper understanding of Wordsworth's strictures on the poetry of the preceding period. How closely his view of social vanity follows that of Pope can be judged by reading Wordsworth's finest portrait of it in *The Prelude* (VII, 551–61); he is describing a preacher in a London church:

> There have I seen a comely bachelor,
> Fresh from a toilette of two hours, ascend
> His rostrum, with seraphic glance look up,
> And, in a tone elaborately low
> Beginning, lead his voice through many a maze
> A minuet course; and, winding up his mouth,
> From time to time, into an orifice
> Most delicate, a lurking eyelet, small,
> And only not invisible, again
> Open it out, diffusing thence a smile
> Of rapt irradiation, exquisite.

That passage from Wordsworth's *Prelude* is not merely an exquisite portrait of social vanity, it is *Rape of the Lock* Pope in blank verse. Although, I suppose, one's immediate thought is that Wordsworth's comely bachelor has his natural setting in the chapel of Pope's fourth *Moral Essay* (141–50):

> And now the chapel's silver bell you hear
> That summons you to all the pride of prayer:
> Light quirks of music, broken and uneven,
> Make the soul dance upon a jig to Heaven.
> On painted ceilings you devoutly stare,
> Where sprawl the saints of Verrio or Laguerre,
> On gilded clouds in fair expansion lie
> And bring all Paradise before your eye.
> To rest, the cushion and soft Dean invite,
> Who never mentions Hell to ears polite.

But the connection between the poetry of Wordsworth and Pope is not merely that Wordsworth is providing a delicious portrait of Pope's 'soft Dean' or that Wordsworth's comely bachelor requires to be set in Pope's chapel. The connection is essentially a poetic one and lies in the manner in which a highly polite language is used to achieve a delicate and wicked irony. Indeed, in a comparison of these two passages. Wordsworth's language will be seen to be far more polite, refined and polished than Pope's and to achieve a far more delicate and sophisticated humour than Pope's.

Wordsworth's strictures, then, are not at the expense of the great achievement of eighteenth-century poetry; as I have tried to show, he can be seen to carry forward these achievements in his own poetry. His strictures are against that 'mere mechanic art' which was bringing the achievements of the eighteenth century into disrepute and was killing poetry at the root.

Wordsworth's appeal against this, as expressed in the preface to *Lyrical Ballads* and the appendix on Poetic Diction, whilst it was essentially a liberating one, and was certainly prompted by a genuine appreciation of the current plight of poetry, was nevertheless limited in its critical understanding. Fundamentally, Wordsworth's appeal was for the straight employment of common speech, rather than for attention to the requirements of the spoken language, to speech rhythms and syntax. A certain critical crudity in Wordsworth's position has been generally recognized, but it has usually been seen in the wrong places. For example, Wordsworth's claim that metre is not necessary to poetry may be thought a case of critical excess, of Wordsworthian overstatement.

But Wordsworth is nevertheless correct: in English, speech rhythms are non-metrical and yet are sufficient for poetry, as witness the poetry of Gerard Manley Hopkins and so much of Shakespeare's mature 'blank verse'. Coleridge actually attacked Wordsworth's claim that metre was unnecessary to poetry and it is significant that Wordsworth did not defend himself by appealing to speech rhythm. It is significant because, in view of his claim to be intent upon 'the language really used by men' his failure to refer to the rhythms of speech indicates that he had not really thought through what was implied in 'returning poetry to the prose order', i.e. to 'the language really used by men'.

Turning from the Preface to *Lyrical Ballads* to the Appendix on Poetic Diction, a similar lack of consideration is apparent. It becomes evident as one reads through the Appendix that Wordsworth had failed to understand the value and the role of poetic diction and decorum in a poetry whose address and values were necessarily public. He fails, most importantly, to realize that diction is a matter of decorum. In his own poetry, inattentiveness to decorum, to making the language conform to the occasion, is noticeable in the notorious bathos of those lines from *Simon Lee*,

> And still, the more he works, the more
> Do his weak ankles swell.

Pope would have spotted the bathos immediately; it arises from a syntax which gives to the revelation of Simon's swollen, weak ankles the air of an official declaration. Elsewhere in Wordsworth's poetry the same inattentiveness prompts him to follow some of the worst excesses of eighteenth-century poetic diction, as (for example) when he refers to a kilt as a 'plaided vest' or, worse still, when he avoids describing a woman as pregnant by referring to her as 'the thankful captive of maternal bonds'! Such circumlocutions are as ludicrous as anyone could hope to discover in eighteenth-century poetry. There is, however, at least one occasion when Wordsworth makes a proper use of poetic diction, or circumlocution; an occasion when he clearly appreciates that diction is a matter of decorum. In *The Prelude*, Wordsworth gives his poetic account of his arrival as an undergraduate in Cambridge. Obviously, this was a great event, an important and awe-inspiring moment, as he reveals in his account of it. This feeling communicates itself to the language and, instead of arriving in Cambridge in something as everyday and run-of-the-mill as a stagecoach, we are told that he arrived in 'an itinerant vehicle'.

Whilst, then, Wordsworth's criticism of the 'mere mechanic art' of much contemporary poetry was liberating, it was not without its limitations, limitations not only in Wordsworth's own critical understanding of diction and decorum but also in his own practice as a poet. Much the same point may be made about Wordsworth's conception of the origin, nature and purpose of poetry. What is, perhaps, most striking about Wordsworth's theoretical position with regards to the origin, nature and purpose of poetry is that it expresses quite an intense individualism. In its origin, he maintains, 'poetry is the spontaneous overflow of powerful feelings' brought to order by the poet as 'emotion recollected in tranquillity'. Poetry, it will be noticed, is not here what it would have been to any previous period, a liberating genre; it is an internal condition of the individual, a state of sensibility rather than a type of literature. And this kind of redefinition of poetry gives rise to the notion of the poetic individual and to a stereotype of the poet as a man obsessed with powerful feelings and acute sensibility. It is a view of the poet as daemonic (a cross betwen Coleridge's daemon lover and the Byronic hero) which blends easily into the view of the poet as prophet. Coleridge's daemon lover was a wild-eyed creature who had fed on the bread of Paradise. The poet, on this view, whilst he may employ 'the language really used by men', is not as other men; he is elevated above his kind by his possession of visionary powers. His mission is to

> arouse the sensual from their sleep
> of Death, and win the vacant and the vain
> To noble raptures.

Needless to say, Wordsworth's own poetry conforms closely to his own description of poetry. There can be little doubting the powerful feelings in which it originates and Wordsworth's own practice of distancing experience by writing of the past ensures that the emotion is recollected in tranquillity. Indeed, Wordsworth's characteristic tone and mood is reflective:

> Thus far, O Friend! did I, not used to make
> A present joy the matter of a song,
> Pour forth that day my soul in measured strains
> That would not be forgotten, and are here
> Recorded: to the open fields I told
> A prophecy: poetic numbers came

> Spontaneously to clothe in priestly robe
> A renovated spirit singled out,
> Such hope was mine, for holy services.

Not only are the tone and mood of these lines from the beginning of *The Prelude* (I, 46–54) those of remembrance, the lines themselves summarize Wordsworth's own poetic stance. His poetry is not used to make 'A present joy the matter of a song', it relies upon 'emotion recollected in tranquillity'. Nevertheless, it calls upon remembrance of an occasion when Wordsworth experienced 'the spontaneous overflow of powerful feelings', as this passage recollects a time when 'poetic numbers came Spontaneously'. His poetry also reflects a belief in the poet as prophet and seer, a man set apart from other men, as in this passage poetry is felt

> to clothe in priestly robe
> A renovated spirit singled out . . .

And as we read through Wordsworth's poetry we are continuously aware that Wordsworth is a prophet, bringing through his poetry a vision of human naturalness.

So that Wordsworth's definition of the origin, nature and purpose of poetry, like Pope's in *An Essay on Criticism* or Eliot's in his essays, is a definition of his own poetry and in defining poetry as he does he is, in fact, seeking to create the criteria by which his own achievement is to be judged.

What I have said of Wordsworth so far underestimates or is likely to lead to an underestimation of his achievement. His occasional descents into the ludicrous –

> I've measured it from side to side:
> 'Tis three feet long and two feet wide

– are rare rather than occasional, and with that last example I believe I have now almost exhausted them. The only other well known instance I can think of is that pointed out by Coleridge; Wordsworth writing of the daffodils:

> They flash upon the inward eye,
> Which is the bliss of solitude;

> And then my heart with pleasure fills,
> And dances with the daffodils.

In the past too much has been made of these rare lapses in Wordsworth's poetry; in general, if you total them, they amount to little more than a handful and involve no more than breaches of decorum. Shakespeare was guilty of more. Consider, for instance, Troilus working himself up into a full pitch of eloquence as he justifies the rape of Helen:

> It was thought meet
> Paris should do some vengeance on the Greeks:
> Your breath of full consent bellied his sails;
> The seas and winds, – old wranglers, – took a truce,
> And did him service: he touch'd the ports desir'd;
> And for an old aunt, whom the Greeks held captive,
> He brought a Grecian queen, whose youth and freshness
> Wrinkles Apollo's, and makes stale the morning.
> Why keep we her? The Grecians keep our aunt!

What a summary of the Trojan attitude to the rape of Helen, the root of Homer's epic conflict

> – Why keep we her? The Grecians keep our aunt!

I mention the rare Wordsworthian descents not to deflate his achievement but simply to suggest that in this he is no better than Shakespeare: his poetical practice, like his critical stance, is not flawless.

It is as the author of *Tintern Abbey, The Prelude, Michael*, the *Immortality Ode* and the story of Margaret (later incorporated into *The Excursion*) that Wordsworth lays claim to the serious attention reserved for a major poet. It is in this body of poetry that one experiences the awe-inspiring power of Wordsworth's reflection and in his achievement of what has been called 'the egotistical sublime' comes to appreciate his peculiarly isolated supremacy amongst the poets of the Romantic Movement.

The sublimated condition of the ego in Wordsworth's poetry gives to the consciousness informing the poetry a detached and brooding air, distinguishing it in kind and not merely in degree from the fervent and often feverish enslavement to the present moment we meet with in Shelley and Keats. The self-concern, the egotism, of *Tintern Abbey*, for example, is expressed in a concern not for a present self but for an alienated self. The self, the ego, is a self seen from without; a detachment made possible by looking back upon the self across a period of time. The feelings of the self are thereby subjected to a mature understanding and consideration, which places their importance for us as we read through the poem: the poet, in short, is not the victim of his feelings, but an artist making his feelings serve his art. Hence, of course, one's recognition as one reads that Wordsworth is selecting from his past (whether a real or an imaginary past) what suits his present poetical purpose. This artistic detachment and control can be felt in the reflectively composed and collected character of his best verse:

> For I have learned
> To look on nature, not as in the hour
> Of thoughtless youth; but hearing oftentimes
> The still, sad music of humanity,
> Nor harsh nor grating, though of ample power
> To chasten and subdue.

The rhythm of those lines is quite remarkable. Shakespeare and Wordsworth are the only English poets who can give to verse the character and the movement of good prose. And of the two, it seems to me that Wordsworth's blank verse is the superior: there is no other English poet who can express himself so well and yet so naturally in blank verse as Wordsworth. That those lines from *Tintern Abbey* are lines of verse is beyond question, but the rhythm and syntax of the lines is that of good prose. Even Shakespeare, expressing himself in blank verse, has commonly to distort the natural rhythm and syntax of the language to fit the verse order. It is seldom that Wordsworth does so, so complete is his mastery of the natural language and of his characteristically blank verse. Bear those lines from *Tintern Abbey* in mind (or those lines portraying the foppish preacher) when pondering Wordsworth's claim that poetry should employ the language really used by men.

Those lines from *Tintern Abbey* illustrate very well the Wordsworthian detachment. True, the passage is egotistic, in that the poet's inner eye (at least) is ever on himself, he is telling us something about himself —

> For *I* have learned . . .

— but the impressionism of immediate experience is absent: we are in the presence not of an immediate reflex but of a mind, which considers, weighs and judges and which, in the careful poise of the lines themselves, establishes a balanced attitude. Wordsworth is peculiar amongst the Romantics because (to adapt a remark which Dr. Johnson made of Donne) in reading him you are made to think: the poetry itself is a pondering and the response to it addresses itself to the senses through the movements of the mind.

I am aware that what I have been saying so far about Wordsworth may seem rather strange. True, I have glanced at a number of conventional, critical preoccupations: at the programme for poetry set out in the preface to *Lyrical Ballads*; at the strictures upon 'Poetic Diction' in the Appendix to *Lyrical Ballads*; at the half a dozen descents into the ludicrous we discover in Wordsworth's poetry; at the claim that Wordsworth's poetry achieves the egotistical sublime. I have, incidentally, made the unconventional point that Wordsworth has an essential connection with Pope which is overlooked by those who believe he was turning away from the Augustans. However, it might well be thought that the account of Wordsworth so far is somewhat similar to an account of *Paradise Lost* which never mentions Satan.

The popular conception of Wordsworth is that he is a Nature poet and I assume that *Nature* in this popular use refers to that range of objects which fall within the scope of Botany, Zoology and Meteorology, in short, the world untouched by and excluding man. This common view of Wordsworth as a Nature poet is grounded no doubt in the fact that much of his poetry is set (as it were) in the English Lake District. It is not the view which Wordsworth himself proposes; he does not see himself as a poet of the countryside, he declares

> the Mind of Man
> My haunt, and the main region of my song.

I've already suggested that this is how I read Wordsworth's poetry – as pondering, reflective, inhabiting the mind. And the nature with which it is concerned, in *Margaret, Michael, The Prelude*, for example, is not the nature of the flowers, the trees, 'the shapeless rock and hanging precipice', it is human nature, 'the still, sad music of humanity'. As you read through Wordsworth, not piecemeal but wholesale – for like all major poets, Wordsworth is only properly appreciated at length, is at his best at length – the characteristic mood asserts itself, through tone and rhythm rather than statement or allusion. The mood is that of a mind brooding upon its own accumulated experience, sustained by a gentle melancholy, at times a sadness. So that, in this way, through the slow assertion of a mood and the slow, reflective rhythms of the verse, the poetry communicates 'the still, sad music of humanity', as it does in the passage from which that phrase is taken. And this, not nature, is what the poetry is 'about': it propounds a sad and gentle sympathy for the pathetic lot of the isolated – the leech gatherer, Margaret, Michael, Simon Lee – and an equally sad but slightly more bitter sympathy for the lot of the crowd, the bustling populace of the city. So that, although we have learned to look upon Wordsworth as a poet of the countryside, his poetry declares him to be, as much as Pope ever was, a poet of the human community and as such the central vision of Wordsworth is urban and not rural. He is, in fact, one of England's finest poets of urban life. This is not the view commonly taken of Wordsworth. The common view of Wordsworth is that his poetry is generally and importantly focused upon the countryside and the world of natural objects. Wordsworth, as I intimated, is not well seved by this reputation, if only because it presents a far narrower definition of his poetic range than the one provided by the poetry itself. The common view certainly does not prepare us for the witty, sophisticated and urbane portrait of the 'comely bachelor' preacher of Book VII of *The Prelude*. The common view also obscures a talent at the opposite extreme from that of witty sophistication and urbanity; it is a talent well represented by the opening of *Peter Bell*:

> There's something in a flying horse,
> There's something in a huge balloon;
> But through the clouds I'll never float
> Until I have a little boat,
> Shaped like the crescent-moon.

The lines have no great poetic merit, but they do represent Wordsworth in a deliberately playful mood, writing what could easily be mistaken for verse-for-children.

These two instances, from Book VII of *The Prelude* and the opening of *Peter Bell*, suggest something of the range of Wordsworth's poetry and my point is that this is not something we are prepared for by the common view of Wordsworth. More precisely, however, my point is that this view does not prepare the reader for the essentially urban poetry of Wordsworth. Indeed, the usual presumption, which places his achievement within the ambit of interest marked out by the poem on the daffodils and the first book of *The Prelude*, actually prevents any serious and sustained interest in areas of more substantial achievement.

The particular area I wish to draw attention to is the one so magnificently marked out in Book VII of *The Prelude*, 'Residence in London'. I wish to do so firstly to continue to correct what I have been calling 'the common view' of Wordsworth, secondly to correct a generally-held critical view of Wordsworth and thirdly, of course, to promote a greater interest in Book VII of *The Prelude* and so in Wordsworth's considerable achievement as an urban poet.

I have already said enough about the 'common view' of Wordsworth to make it unnecessary to say more. It insists that he is the poet of mountains, trees and flowers, a poet of the country landscape. This in itself disprizes his poetry by diminishing its range, tone and mood. This view is confirmed by a great deal of criticism, which represents Wordsworth as a refugee from the city and the busy haunts of men. The keynote to this critical strain is provided, I suppose, by the original (1805) opening of *The Prelude*:

> O welcome, messenger! O welcome, friend!
> A captive greets thee, coming from a house of bondage,
> From yon city walls set free.

That strain is by no means uncommon in Wordsworth's poetry and it is evident enough that Wordsworth was highly critical of city life. In the poem *Michael*, for instance, we learn that Michael's son, Luke, 'in the dissolute city gave himself to evil courses'.

There is, therefore, some substance in the view which presents Wordsworth to us as a poet who fled from the constraint and corruption of the city to the honesty and freedom of the countryside. This in itself however, does not make Wordsworth any less an urban poet than, say, Horace. The Roman poet also opposed city corruption to rural honesty, but it would be a strange opinion of Horace which held him to be a 'nature' poet. Whether a poet is an urban poet or not does not depend upon his view of the city and city life. An analogy might be drawn here with the city-dweller: many city dwellers could utter those original opening lines of *The Prelude* as they flee from the city on weekends, but the fact that they look upon the city as a place of bondage and that they consider a sojourn in the countryside to be rejuvenating and revitalizing, doesn't make them any the less city dwellers. Indeed, it might be said that such an attitude to the countryside is peculiarly urban. It will be noticed, on a reading of *The Prelude*, that Wordsworth himself is well aware that his residence in the city, whether London, Paris or Cambridge, has been instrumental in fashioning his own peculiar mystique of country life and in forming his opinions of its unique moral benefits.

But whilst Wordsworth's attitude to the city and city life is not relevant to his standing as an urban poet, it might be as well to correct the one-sided view of this attitude that is so widely prevalent. When Wordsworth writes of the city, he does not invariably represent it as a prison or as a place of corruption. Here, for instance, is a view of London, 'Composed [as the title of the sonnet tells us] upon Westminster Bridge, September 3, 1802' – although actually composed [so the note tells us] on July 31, 1802:

> Earth has not anything to show more fair:
> Dull would he be of soul who could pass by
> A sight so touching in its majesty:
> This City now doth, like a garment, wear
> The beauty of the morning; silent, bare,
> Ships, towers, domes, theatres, and temples lie
> Open unto the fields, and to the sky;
> All bright and glittering in the smokeless air.
> Never did sun more beautifully steep
> In his first splendour, valley, rock, or hill;
> Ne'er saw I, never felt, a calm so deep!
> The river glideth at his own sweet will:
> Dear God! the very houses seem asleep;
> And all that mighty heart is lying still.

When confronted with so much that is written of Wordsworth, we do well to recall this sonnet. It is true that Wordsworth was deeply moved by the beauty of natural scenery, but no more so than he was moved by the beauty of the city of London; indeed, he places the beauty of the city on a par with that of natural scenery, at least by implication, when he declares that

> Earth has not anything to show more fair

and goes on to claim that

> Never did sun more beautifully steep
> In his first splendour, valley, rock, or hill.

It is equally true that Wordsworth more than most, or more articulately than most, experienced the healing calm of natural surroundings. But, again, the calm which he experienced on viewing the city was a far deeper calm than that, as he acknowledges:

> Ne'er saw I, never felt, a calm so deep!

Similarly, one can match from this sonnet Wordsworth's sense of the power of nature with his similar sense of the power of the city. Here London lies like a sleeping giant:

> And all that mighty heart is lying still.

So, much that is said of Wordsworth's response to the calm, the beauty and the power of natural objects can with equal relevance be said of his response to the city in the sonnet composed upon Westminster Bridge. No doubt it will be objected that the sonnet doesn't permit a fair comparison, simply because it praises a *sleeping* city. Now, I must admit, that seems to me a fair objection: in the sonnet, the city is uncharacteristic – it is silent, still, peaceful and not the busy, bustling place we normally think of as a city. But what are we to conclude from this? That the sonnet cannot be taken as expressing Wordsworth's opinions of the city? But if it doesn't express an opinion of the city, what does it express an opinion of? Surely, the point is that the sonnet *does* express Wordsworth's view of the city and the peculiarity of it is that it catches London on an occasion when it is possible to distinguish the city from city life.

Now that might tempt the critic to say, 'Ah, yes! Wordsworth admired London, but he strongly disapproved of the life of the city. It was city life that he considered dissolute.' But, unfortunately, the critic cannot even take that comfort from the sonnet without doing it some injustice; some weight has to be given to the final line of the sonnet, if for no other reason than that it is the final line:

> And all that mighty heart is lying still.

The implicit view of city life contained in that reference to the mighty heart is by no means as simple as that of the critic who wishes to believe that Wordsworth saw city life as dissolute: the emphasis is upon power, not upon dissolution; it communicates a certain admiration – although, of course, Wordsworth may have believed that that power was a power for evil. If he did believe that, then his attitude towards it in the phrase 'mighty heart' is as ambiguous as Milton's attitude to Satan and Dryden's attitude to Shaftesbury. One can admire the power without admiring the ends to which it is put.

In Book VII of *The Prelude*, 'Residence in London', Wordsworth's view of the city is less remote than in the sonnet; here he takes us into the heart of the city, that 'mighty heart' which 'is lying still' in the sonnet. Initially, the view of the city, now awake and bustling with activity, is such as would confirm the opinion of those who believe Wordsworth was antagonistic to city life. London is here described as a 'monstrous ant-hill on the plain of a too busy world'.

The 'monstrous ant-hill on the plain of a too busy world', however, provides only a distant prospect of the bustling city and the judgement contained in the metaphor consequently appears somewhat remote. It is a judgement which becomes almost impertinent as the poem comes to closer grips with the activity of the city:

> The quick dance
> Of colours, lights, and forms; the deafening din;
> The comers and the goers face to face,
> Face after face; the string of dazzling wares,
> Shop after shop, with symbols, blazoned names,
> And all the tradesman's honours overhead:
> Here, fronts of houses, like a title-page,
> With letters huge inscribed from top to toe; &c.

Wordsworth's usual pace is slow, deliberate; it is the pace of the pondering, reflective mind. Here, however, the poetry changes gear and we move by a gradual transition from the characteristic Wordsworthian rhythm of

> Rise up, thou monstrous ant-hill on the plain
> Of a too busy world! Before me flow,
> Thou endless stream of men and moving things!

To what (as the stream begins to flow) the lines themselves call 'the quick dance'. The effect

> Of colours, lights, and forms . . .
> The comers and the goers face to face,
> Face after face; the string of dazzling wares,
> Shop after shop, with symbols, blazoned names . . .

The effect is of considerable speed, of a busy street seen from a moving train. The consequence of the speed with which the images seem to flash past is one of mounting excitement. It is that sense of movement and the excitement it records and creates which defines Wordsworth's attitude to the teeming life of London.

That the city teems with life carries its own implication, felt rather than formulated in passages such as those which describe the street entertainers and other characters:

> A raree-show is here,
> With children gathered round; another street
> Presents a company of dancing dogs,
> Or dromedary, with an antic pair
> Of monkeys on his back; a minstrel band
> Of Savoyards; or, single and alone,
> An English ballad-singer . . .

A little later:

> A travelling cripple, by the trunk cut short,
> And stumping on his arms. In sailor's garb
> Another lies at length, beside a range
> Of well-formed characters, with chalk inscribed
> Upon the smooth flat stones: the Nurse is here,
> The Bachelor, that loves to sun himself,
> The military Idler, and the Dame,
> That field-ward takes her walk with decent steps.
>   Now homeward through the thickening hubbub, where
> See, among less distinguishable shapes,
> The begging scavenger, with hat in hand;
> The Italian, as he thrids his way with care,
> Steadying, far-seen, a frame of images
> Upon his head; with basket at his breast
> The Jew; the stately and slow-moving Turk,
> With freight of slippers piled beneath his arm!

> Enough; – the mighty concourse I surveyed
> With no unthinking mind, well pleased to note
> Among the crowd all specimens of man,
> Through all the colours which the sun bestows,
> And every character of form and face:
> The Swede, the Russian; from the genial south,
> The Frenchman and the Spaniard; from remote
> America, the Hunter–Indian; Moors,
> Malays, Lascars, the Tartar, the Chinese,
> And Negro ladies in white muslin gowns.

The quotation is lengthy, but even so it expresses only some small part of the experience of a walk through London, which provides the substance of Book VII. The compound image of a busy, entertaining, multi-racial community which is created as we read is one which conveys a greater pleasure, interest and excitement than we are led to expect from the initial description of the city as a 'monstrous ant-hill on the plain of a too busy world'.

What overturns that initial judgement of the city is the poem's obvious fascination with the 'mighty concourse', a fascination which nicely dissolves the crowd into a series of individual characters:

> Single and alone,
> An English ballad singer . . .
> the Dame,
> That field-ward takes her walk with decent steps . . .
> The Italian, as he thrids his way with care . . .
> the stately and slow-moving Turk,
> With freight of slippers piled beneath his arm!

And perhaps to us the most interesting of these, the 'Negro ladies in white muslin gowns'. In its attitude to the multi-racial community –

> well pleased to note
> Among the crowd all specimens of man . . .

– and in that reference to 'Negro ladies', which in the era of English slave-trading affords the negro respect and dignity, the poem communicates an appreciation of the teeming, cosmopolitan masses of the city quite at odds with that which we are led to expect by the

common view of Wordsworth. City life may be dissolute, as it is
presented in *Michael*, it may also be marred by

> A travelling cripple, by the trunk cut short,
> And stumping on his arms

and by

> The begging scavenger, with hat in hand,

but it is also the home of

> the Dame,
> That field-ward takes her walk with *decent* steps,
> the *stately* and slow-moving Turk
> And Negro *ladies* in white muslin gowns.

In short, the Wordsworthian city has its virtues as well as its vices, its
beauties as well as its blemishes; it is morally and aesthetically as well as
racially variegated. And the poem 'Residence in London' creates a
magnificent sense of the rich variety, vitality and density of life in a
metropolis.

The sense of variety and density of life is produced not merely by
descriptions of the crowds; it is created often by subtle and yet powerful
contrasts between things seen as the narrator walks about the city.
Having, for instance, meandered through the Inns of Court, where
'studious lawyers look out on waters, walks, and gardens green', the
narrator turns again to the busy streets:

> Thence back into the throng, until we reach
> Following the tide that slackens by degrees,
> Some half-frequented scene, where wider streets
> Bring straggling breezes of suburban air.
> Here files of ballads dangle from dead walls;
> Advertisements, of giant size, from high
> Press forward, in all colours, on the sight . . .

It is worth noticing here Wordsworth's use of rhythm to enact his
meaning – what is called 'the dramatic use of rhythm'. Notice the tight-
packed clause, 'Thence back into the throng' and compare it with the

more leisurely and spacious one, 'where wider streets Bring straggling breezes of suburban air.' The first is as packed as the throng and as abrupt as the movement into the crowd; the second is as leisured as the 'straggling breezes' and as expansive as the 'wider streets'. That is one type of contrast, creating surreptitiously our awareness of the variety of life. Another is that contained in the last three lines of the passage:

> Here files of ballads dangle from dead walls;
> Advertisements, of giant size, from high
> Press forward, in all colours, on the sight . . .

The ballads *dangle*, the word suggests lifeless, from *dead* walls: the whole line implies deadness, dullness, a lack of energy. In contrast, the advertisements are clamorous, vigorous, overpowering: they are 'of giant size' and 'from high Press forward, in all colours'. Once again, the surreptitious contrast adds to our sense of the variegations of urban experience.

Incidentally, it is perhaps worth remarking the peculiarly contemporary cultural comment implicit in this last contrast, in which the ballads hang neglected and giant advertisements divert and capture the attention. Much the same irony is marked by the earlier contrast between the raree show 'with children gathered round' and 'single and alone, An English ballad-singer'. *Irony* may seem too strong and deliberate a term to describes such contrasts and yet, particularly in the case of the files of ballads and the advertisements, the contrast is too deliberate to allow a weaker or less pointed response. And what, of course, gives the implicit comment upon the state of popular culture its special edge is the recollection that Wordsworth himself began his poetical career as a balladeer, in *Lyrical Ballads*. Unlike Eliot in *The Waste Land*, however, Wordsworth is not a cultural snob; where Eliot assumes his own cultural superiority in order to demean and to make fun of 'the low', in the pub scene and in the typist scene for instance, Wordsworth does not withhold his sympathies from the 'popular'. His attitude towards the depreciation of popular culture is not a superior sneer but a momentary sadness, present in the tone of such lines as

> or, single and alone,
> An English ballad-singer

and

Here files of ballads dangle from dead walls.

And it is in tone, hence attitude, and not only in technique, in his dramatic presentation of city life, that Wordsworth stands superior to Eliot as an urban poet.

I mention Eliot by way of comparison, because he is – at least by repute – the greatest urban poet of our own times, at least the greatest English urban poet of our times. As one reads through the poetry of the twentieth century, it is not difficult to understand why Eliot should be so highly regarded. He is, without a doubt, the first to write in the language of the twentieth century, in a language really used by twentieth-century men. It is, however, a rather special and peculiar language; the bored conversational language of the smart, cocktail set of the 'twenties and it expresses the values of that set very well: it is hoity-toity, given to cultural name-dropping and quotation, full of contempt for the vulgar, the popular, and it is racist, more particularly, anti-semitic. It is, in short, all very smart with the smartness of the 'twenties. In its attitude to urban life, Eliot's poetry is one of profound and snooty distaste: city-dwellers are mindless automatons and the city is arid, seedy and disgusting. Wordsworth's view of the city is wider, richer, more profound and consequently more human than Eliot's. One's experience of Eliot's poetry is of a vision nastily blinkered by prejudice, as in his reference to the Jew 'spawned in some estaminet in Antwerp', where Wordsworth's poetry escapes the prejudices of its time, as when it refers to 'Negro ladies in white muslin gowns'. It is this breadth of vision, one which Wordsworth shared with Shakespeare (as witness Shylock), that enables Wordsworth to create an awareness of city life beyond the scope and range of Eliot. No city so populated with people and so crowded with multifarious experience as Wordsworth's city is could be the Waste Land into which Eliot's narrower and meaner vision contracts it. It is in his ability to create the variety of urban experience that Wordsworth stands superior to Eliot, no less than in his moral vision of the throng.

I mentioned Shakespeare and from time to time, as one reads through Book VII of *The Prelude*, the acquaintance between Wordsworth and Shakespeare appears more than casual or coincidental. It is not merely prompted by a similarity in the blank verse – in general, Wordsworth's blank verse is superior to Shakespeare's – nor is it that there is any suggestion that Wordsworth is imitating Shakespeare; it is rather that, where one can judge, Wordsworth's poetry has the same dramatic power as Shakespeare's. Perhaps it isn't entirely fortuitous that the most obvious instance of this in 'Residence in London' is a description of a character in a play:

> A scare-crow pattern of old age dressed up
> In all the tatters of infirmity
> All loosely put together, hobbled in,
> Stumping upon a cane with which he smites,
> From time to time, the solid boards, and makes them
> Prate somewhat loudly of the whereabouts
> Of one so overloaded with his years.

Smites and *prate* give the lines an antique air, but they don't bring Shakespeare particularly to mind: they serve simply to point up the antiquity of the character – that and the fact that he is a character in some old drama. Linguistically, what is reminiscent of Shakespeare is a certain vernacular turn of phrase – 'the tatters of infirmity', 'hobbled in', 'Stumping upon a cane'. These phrases give substance to the presence of the character; a process of realization which is ably furthered by Wordsworth's own feeling for the vernacular, in such expressions as 'A scare-crow pattern of old age dressed up' and 'All loosely put together'.

Nothing that I've said of Wordsworth so far has anything to do with his 'philosophy of Nature'. I have considered Wordsworth in much the same way as that other great narrative poet, Chaucer, is considered. Indeed, I may well have given the impression that 'Residence in London' is a kind of latter-day 'General Prologue', in which the narrator's perambulation through the city is similar to the narrator's perambulation in Chaucer and Wordsworth's insight communicated, like Chaucer's in the Prologue, through a series of portraits and descriptions of objects. If that is the impression received, then it is a good one: even the instance of irony I mentioned is somewhat Chaucerian, operating by juxtaposition, by placing the dangling ballads beside the pressing advertisements and allowing the companionship of the two to be its own comment. The portrait of the 'comely bachelor' preacher, likewise, has its obvious ancestor in Chaucer's portrait of the Prioress, and the irony of both portraits has the same generation, in implicit inappropriateness.

The reason for associating Wordsworth with Chaucer – as with Pope and Shakespeare – is to transform the attention given to his poetry as we read it. It is intended to draw attention away from the abstraction of interest marked by a concern for his 'philosophy of nature' and to

concentrate it instead upon the real medium through which
Wordsworth humanized nature and naturalized humanity: the actual
passages in which he realized his haunting consciousness of 'the music of
humanity', not always – as I've tried to show – a 'still, sad music', but in
the 'mighty heart' of the city sometimes as stately as the 'stately Turk'
and as dignified as the 'Negro ladies in white muslin gowns'. It has been
my intention to suggest that nowhere in Wordsworth's poetry is his
sense of 'the music of humanity' better orchestrated than in his urban
poetry, where the human fabric of life has greater density, richness and
variety than is dreamt of in Wordsworth's 'philosophy'. Whilst
Wordsworth does distinguish between 'the mean and vulgar works of
man' and what he calls 'high objects', namely the manifestation of
Nature, the distinction is somewhat misleading, since it fails to represent
the actual character of Wordsworth's dealings with Nature in the poetry
itself. Consideration of some of the famous passages from *The Prelude*
will illustrate this, I hope, and also indicate the justice of Wordsworth's
comment,

> The mind of man,
> The haunt and main region of my song.

The first of these passages occurs in Book I of *The Prelude*, 'Childhood
and School-Time'. It is a lengthy passage and there seems no alternative
to quoting it in full. In reading it, notice how well Wordsworth can
create the atmosphere required: the initially hushed and leisurely
movement, as the boat moves

> Leaving behind her still, on either side,
> Small circles glittering idly in the moon . . . ;

the sudden, awesome power of the mountain,

> When, from behind the craggy steep, till then
> The horizon's bound, a huge peak, black and huge,
> As if with voluntary power instinct
> Upreared its head . . . ;

and finally, how in the conclusion the syntax and the movement of the
lines seems to capture the haunted consciousness of the child –

>   for many days, my brain
> Worked with a dim and undetermined sense
> Of unknown modes of being; o'er my thoughts
> There hung a darkness, call it solitude
> Or blank desertion. No familiar shapes
> Remained, no pleasant images of trees,
> Of sea or sky, no colours of green fields;
> But huge and mighty forms, that do not live
> Like living men, moved slowly through the mind
> By day, and were a trouble to my dreams.

The passage, then, is not merely a narrative passage, it realizes and so makes dramatically present to us the experiences narrated. The passage is usually referred to as 'the stolen boat passage'.

> One summer evening (led by her [i.e. Nature]) I found
> A little boat tied to a willow tree
> Within a rocky cave, its usual home.
> Straight I unloosed her chain, and stepping in
> Pushed from the shore. It was an act of stealth
> And troubled pleasure, not without the voice
> Of mountain-echoes did my boat move on;
> Leaving behind her still, on either side,
> Small circles glittering idly in the moon,
> Until they melted all into one track
> Of sparkling light. But now, like one who rows,
> Proud of his skill, to reach a chosen point
> With an unswerving line, I fixed my view
> Upon the summit of a craggy ridge,
> The horizon's utmost boundary; for above
> Was nothing but the stars and the grey sky.
> She was an elfin pinnace; lustily
> I dipped my oars into the silent lake,
> And, as I rose upon the stroke, my boat
> Went heaving through the water like a swan;
> When, from behind that craggy steep till then
> The horizon's bound, a huge peak, black and huge,
> As if with voluntary power instinct
> Upreared its head. I struck and struck again,
> And growing still in stature the grim shape

Towered up between me and the stars, and still,
For so it seemed, with purpose of its own
And measured motion like a living thing,
Strode after me, With trembling oars I turned,
And through the silent water stole my way
Back to the covert of the willow tree;
There in her mooring-place I left my bark, –
And through the meadows went, in grave
And serious mood; but after I had seen
That spectacle, for many days, my brain
Worked with a dim and undetermined sense
Of unknown modes of being; o'er my thoughts
There hung a darkness, call it solitude
Or blank desertion. No familiar shapes
Remained, no pleasant images of trees,
Of sea or sky, no colours of green fields;
But huge and mighty forms, that do not live
Like living men, moved slowly through the mind
By day, and were a trouble to my dreams.

Although what is happening here appears mysterious at first, it is evident that Wordsworth is describing an actual experience: I take this to be so, simply because the optical illusion it reports is somewhat complicated but quite natural. As the boat pulls away from the bank more and more of the peak beyond becomes visible, creating the illusion that it is rising up and threatening the child in the boat.

  The passage illustrates rather well Wordsworth's belief in Nature as a powerful, educative, moral force. The child described in the passage has done wrong, he has stolen a boat, for which he is immediately admonished by Nature, as the peak rises above him like an irate adult. The experience has a powerful effect upon the psychology of the child:

              O'er my thoughts
      There hung a darkness, call it solitude
      Or blank desertion . . .
                    huge and mighty forms, that do not live
      Like living men, moved slowly through the mind
      By day, and were a trouble to my dreams.

It is through this kind of pyschological shock-therapy that Nature is active in shaping the moral consciousness of those available to its influences. This belief is summed up by Wordsworth in the stanza of a smaller poem:

> One impulse from a vernal wood
> Can teach you more of man,
> Of moral evil and of good
> Than all the sages can.

And certainly, in the 'stolen boat' passage, one impulse from the peak is felt to have taught the child a profounder moral lesson than any scolding by his elders would have done.

Nature provides the same moral education to the child who takes the catch from traps laid by someone else:

> Sometimes it befell
> In these night wanderings, that a strong desire
> O'erpowered my better reason, and the bird
> Which was the captive of another's toil
> Became my prey; and when the deed was done
> I heard among the solitary hills
> Low breathings coming after me, and sounds
> Of undistinguishable motion, steps
> Almost as silent as the turf they trod.

Nowadays, we would have some doubts about the use of fear as an instrument of moral instruction and may wonder, as we consider these illustrations from the first book of *The Prelude*, whether Nature hasn't simply assumed the role of the bogey man.

The point I wished to make, however, has nothing to do with educational method: it is that for Wordsworth, as for the medieval schoolmen, for Shakespeare and for Pope, Nature is a moral force and not flowers, trees, and mountains. And whilst a flower may exist as a thing-in-itself, unperceived by and unbeknown to man, Nature as a moral force exists only as a human experience. This is evident in the passages quoted from *The Prelude*, where the sense of Nature as a moral force is illustrated. The towering threat of the peak and the 'low breathings' coming from 'the solitary hills' are experiences and not things-in-themselves; they would not exist, that is to say, unless they were perceived, since they are perceptions – or, more narrowly, one might say that they are psychological effects and, as such, do not and cannot exist outside and apart from the human psyche.

In fact, as one reads the passages in which Wordsworth presents the workings of Nature to the reader of *The Prelude*, it becomes increasingly evident that these workings are psychological ones. The forms of Nature, which mould the moral consciousness, though prompted (as it were) by the observation of natural objects, are (as they are described in the 'stolen boat' passage),

> huge and mighty forms, that do not live
> Like living men [but which] moved slowly through the mind
> By day, and were a trouble to my dreams.

In short, the mountains which we have in view here are not those of the Lake District, but belong to the landscape of the mind. They might best be compared with those of Gerard Manley Hopkins' sonnet, 'No worst, there is none', where we are reminded that there is a mental landscape:

> O the mind, mind has mountains; cliffs of fall
> Frightful, sheer, no-man-fathomed. Hold them cheap
> May who ne'er hung there.

And, in the same way, the motions of Nature become in Wordsworth movements in the mind, as in the case of the towering, striding peak of the 'stolen boat' passage or, in the same book of *The Prelude*, the whirling motion of the hills in the skating passage:

> and oftentimes,
> When we had given our bodies to the wind,
> And all the shadowy banks on either side
> Came sweeping through the darkness, spinning still
> The rapid line of motion, then at once
> Have I, reclining back upon my heels,
> Stopped short; yet still the solitary cliffs
> Wheeled by me – even as if the earth had rolled
> With visible motion her diurnal round!
> Behind me did they stretch in solemn train,
> Feebler and feebler, and I stood and watched
> Till all was tranquil as a dreamless sleep.

The movement of the cliffs here is merely psychological, a consequence of the skater's dizziness: they move only in his mind.

It has often been remarked, of course, that Wordsworth's Nature is peculiarly animated; that it seems to be, in Wordsworth's own phrase, 'with voluntary power instinct' and therefore to have the characteristics of a living being. As one reads the particular passages which lend support to this view and create this impression, these characteristics are revealed to us as psychological ones and the voluntary power which they seem to possess appears as a power of the mind. In short, Wordsworth emerges as a poet not of Nature-out-there but as a poet of Nature-in-here, a poet of human nature, intent upon the education of consciousness through the workings of the mind. Hence the subtitle of *The Prelude* – 'Growth of a Poet's Mind'. More significantly, the direction of interest is apparent in the words of the poem itself, in such lines as:

> sedulous as I have been to trace
> How Nature by extrinsic passion first
> Peopled the mind with forms sublime or fair,
> And made me love them . . .

The love, it will be noticed, is for the inhabitants of the mind and not for the objects of the extrinsic passion which caused them to take up their dwelling in the mind.

In Wordsworth's poetry, then, Nature, which we too commonly think of as an external force inhabiting a world of natural objects, becomes a psychological force inhabiting the mind of man. Though others may not have grasped this as the matter of Wordsworth's poetry, Wordsworth himself did and did so quite explicitly when he called 'The mind of man, the haunt and the main region of my song'.

Taking the point, then, that Wordsworth's poetry is essentially psychological and that its central concern is for the landscape and the workings of the mind, we become more fully aware of Wordsworth's distinction between 'the mean and vulgar works of man' and 'high objects', such as are the manifestations of Nature. The distinction which Wordsworth is making is not one between the human and the natural, for (as we have seen) the nature which Wordsworth celebrates is human nature and his 'high objects' are those 'forms sublime or fair' which people the mind. Furthermore, as I tried to indicate in looking at the sonnet 'Composed on Westminster Bridge', no absolute sense can be given to Wordsworth's description of the works of man as 'mean and vulgar'; on the contrary, according the Wordsworth, 'Earth has not anything to show more fair'. Finally, a reading of Wordsworth's magnificent urban poem, 'Residence in London', reveals to us a mind and sensibility in sympathy with urban experience and 'the works of man' from which this is compounded.

What, then, are we to make of Wordsworth's own distinction between 'high objects' and 'the mean and vulgar works of man'? My own belief is that one answers this question very readily, even if one does not formulate or articulate the answer, as one reads through Wordsworth's poetry. The sense which the poetry of Wordsworth communicates is not an aesthetic one: one's response to the landscape, that is to the extrinsic landscape, is not in terms of its beauty or its ugliness – 'How sweet the daffodils of spring'. The reader's response is carefully created by Wordsworth; one becomes increasingly aware in *The Prelude*, for instance, that what is being undertaken is a work of psycho-analysis, an attempt to trace a present state of consciousness right back to its source in the early days of childhood. Again, Wordsworth was well aware of this; in the *Ode on Intimations of Immortality* he announces an opinion which could well have been taken as the slogan of Freudianism, when he remarks that 'The child is father to the man'. *The Prelude*, therefore, sets out as an attempt to understand the adult mind in terms of the formative experiences of childhood, such as are recalled in the 'stolen boat' passage and the 'stolen birds' passage.

We are aware of this as we read, although we may not actually formulate this awareness. But it is not our ultimate awareness of the direction of interest in the poetry. We are, for instance, aware (in some sense) of the psychological nature of the experience which is being created in the 'stolen boat' passage; we are aware that it is in some indeterminate way a traumatic experience and that as such it has a powerful, dark and haunting effect upon the formative consciousness of the child. All of that is something we are aware of in some sense as we read. However, our ultimate awareness is not of the psychological experience but of the moral one. The impulse of the child in stealing the boat and the impulse which animates the peak is like the 'impulse from the vernal wood' in the stanza quoted earlier; the impulses here are 'of moral evil and of good'. The consciousness that is being formed is a moral consciousness, so that the psychological force of Wordsworth's poetry makes itself felt ultimately as a moral force. Put very crudely, Wordsworth's poetry is ultimately intent upon how people should behave towards each other and what those two passages from Book I of

The Prelude teach (as it were) is the commandment 'Thou shalt not steal'. That is a very crude way of putting it; however, it serves to make the point that Wordsworth's poetry does not merely haunt the mind but does so in a manner which is ultimately moral, which is ultimately intent upon a world of human values.

Wordsworth, then, adopts (to borrow a phrase from Matthew Arnold) 'a central, a truly human point of view'. His poetry is intent not merely upon experiences, powerful though many of its experiences are; it is intent upon the *value* of experiences. Let me refer once again to the instance of the 'stolen boat' passage: the experience created there is a very powerful one, but the passage itself is intent upon the value of that experience and only incidentally upon its power: the power is merely an instrument of the value, the morality, serving to drive home the worth of that particular kind of experience.

So, Wordsworth looks out – upon the city or upon the peaks – and asks (as it were), What is the human significance and the human value of all this? His poetry answers the first of those questions by transforming the outer landscape into a human one, into a landscape of the mind, the second by demonstrating how the formation of that inner landscape affects the development of human consciousness.

The Social World of Jane Austen

'Men,' says Anne Elliott to Captain Harville in *Persuasion*, 'have had every advantage of us in telling their own story. Education has been theirs in so much higher a degree; the pen has been in their hands.' Jane Austen is an exception to the truth of this observation. Although in literature generally the female is little more than an appendage to a masculine world, in her novels the situation is quite the reverse. This is not simply to be explained in terms of characterization, by the fact that events relate most closely to the responses of female characters; it is more largely due to the greater wiles with which the narrative establishes a distinctively feminine insight. Consider, for instance, the account of Sir William Lucas in *Pride and Prejudice*:

> Within a short walk of Longbourn lived a family with whom the Bennets were particularly intimate. Sir William Lucas had been formerly in trade in Meryton, where he had made a tolerable fortune, and risen to the honour of Knighthood by an address to the king during his mayoralty. The distinction had, perhaps, been felt too strongly. It had given him a disgust to his business and to his residence in a small market town; and quitting them both, he had removed with his family to a house about a mile from Meryton, denominated from that period Lucas Lodge; where he could think with pleasure of his own importance, and, unshackled by business, occupy himself solely in being civil to the world. For though elated by his rank, it did not render him supercilious; on the contrary, he was all attention to everybody. By nature inoffensive, friendly, and obliging, his presentation at St. James's had made him courteous.

The barbed appraisal here is that of a gossip of genius, it is subtle, shifting and insidious until eventually, in that last sentence, it is not at all certain whether the narrator is being straightforward or ironic; would a brief visit to St. James's be sufficient to teach Sir William what courtesy is? Isn't the suggestion that since his presentation he likes to think himself courteous?

The shifting implications of Jane Austen's language invariably imply a very sharp eye for the details of social behaviour; a peculiarly feminine accomplishment. There is hardly a narrative appraisal in the novel which does not share in this accomplishment. To carry the point home I turn at random to yet another brief biographical notice, this time of the Bingley sisters:

> They were rather handsome; had been educated in one of the first private seminaries in town; had a fortune of twenty thousand pounds; were in the habit of spending more than they ought, and of associating with people of rank; and were, therefore, in every respect entitled to think well of themselves and meanly of others. They were of a respectable family in the north of England – a circumstance more deeply impressed on their memories than that their brother's fortune and their own had been acquired by trade.

The Bingley sisters are handsome, well-educated, rich, extravagant, and mix in the best circles – so much is straight description; but with the comment, 'and were, therefore, in every respect entitled to think well of themselves and meanly of others', we have a use of language reminiscent of Chaucer's frequent approvals in the General Prologue. The quiet irony here makes its effect felt in the final sentence, a sentence in which apparently straight description becomes tacitly appraising. Again one has the shifting implication of which Jane Austen is the master, or rather mistress, in the English novel.

The femininity of viewpoint revealed in such writing can prove something of a shock to the male ego – and to the female one that has been masculinely nourished; it is a shock from which many readers fail to recover. It is no uncommon remark that Jane Austen's novels are limited because they are centred in a female world – as though that was a greater limitation than that suffered by man-centred novels. It is also common to remark upon the limited scope of Jane Austen's novels, a remark which arises from equating the range of a novel, the variegated intelligence which informs it, with its topographical and sociological scope; as though *Shirley* were a better novel than *Wuthering Heights* because in the former we see more of the world! A moment's reflection should carry conviction that insight, the range and depth of intelligence, is not at all the same as panorama of subject and that at the level at which novels have value it is *Shirley* that suffers from narrowness and *Wuthering Heights* that commands the range only to be met with in a major work.

Such criticisms of Jane Austen can usually be dismissed as irrelevant since, by and large, they are not grounded in any close consideration of the character of the actual writing of the novels and are mere expressions of prejudice. There are, however, points when such criticisms can be brought to bear directly upon 'the words on the page'. A clear instance is that which we meet in Chapter IX of *Pride and Prejudice* where Bingley, Elizabeth and then Darcy are in conversation:

> 'I did not know before,' continued Bingley immediately, 'that you were a studier of character. It must be an amusing study.'
>
> 'Yes; but intricate characters are the *most* amusing. They have at least that advantage.'
>
> 'The country,' said Darcy, 'can in general supply but few subjects for such a study. In a country neighbourhood you move in a very confined and unvarying society.'
>
> 'But people themselves alter so much that there is something new to be observed in them for ever.'

Here the novel meets the charge of limited scope in a brief discussion of character. In response to Elizabeth's declared interest in 'intricate characters' Darcy observes that there are 'few subjects for such a study' in the 'very confined and unvarying society' of 'a country neighbourhood'. That this is not so we already know from the description of Elizabeth's father in the opening chapter:

> Mr. Bennet was so odd a mixture of quick parts, sarcastic humour, reserve, and caprice, that the experience of three-and-twenty years had been insufficient to make his wife understand his character.

In this, it would seem, Mr. Bennet is no more than an extreme case of the general rule advanced by Elizabeth, that 'people themselves alter so much that there is something new to be observed in them for ever'.

In the exchange between Elizabeth and Darcy it is as if Elizabeth, momently, speaking of the observation of characters, does so on behalf of the narrator and ultimately the novelist. It is a peculiar but not a unique intervention of the novelist into the novel. Following the description of Mr. Bennet's character, which has been quoted above, the narrator continues, of Mrs. Bennet, 'Her mind was less difficult to develop'. In that sentence it is the novelist, the developer of characters, and not the narrator who speaks.

That novelists may be aware of the criticism likely to be levelled at their work and, as in Elizabeth's conversation with Darcy, attempt to answer it has not been sufficiently recognized. Charlotte Brontë, for instance, asked for indulgence to be shown to *Wuthering Heights* and pleaded her sister's 'limited experience'. Emily herself, however, had made out her own case, much as Jane Austen does, in the conversation of Lockwood and Nelly Dean. Lockwood confesses to Nelly,

> I perceive that people in these regions acquire over people in towns the value that the spider in a dungeon does over a spider in a cottage, to their various occupants; and yet the deepened attraction is not entirely owing to the situation of the looker-on. They *do* live more in earnest, more in themselves, and less in surface change, and frivolous external things. . . .

That states a claim to deeper seriousness for the situation of the 'looker-on' in *Wuthering Heights*, a claim which Charlotte seems to have overlooked, for the best defence of her sister's novel she could have mounted in 1850 was offered by the Wordsworthian view of rural life expressed in Lockwood's perception.

Where Emily Brontë meets the charge of 'limited experience' by an appeal to profundity, Jane Austen lays claim to complexity. That Jane Austen's novels are narrative studies of character in which intricacy and variety become 'the spice of life' is intimated both in the initial narrative description of Mr. and Mrs. Bennet and in the exchange between Elizabeth and Darcy. In general the variety is created by changes in the narrative point of view and the 'spice' by the 'sarcastic humour' of the narrator. The humour of the narrator is often wickedly feminine and of the type epitomized in the compliment, 'I've always admired the dress you're wearing.' Such is the praise afforded by the narrator to Mrs. Bennet's provisions for her guests, the Gardiners.

> The Gardiners stayed a week at Longbourn; and what with the Philipses, the Lucases, and the officers, there was not a day without its engagement. Mrs. Bennet had so carefully provided for the entertainment of her brother and sister, that they did not once sit down to a family dinner.

Different constructions are being placed upon Mrs. Bennet's care and hospitality by a narrator with a sharp eye for the finer details of social behaviour.

The social nature of Jane Austen's vision is apparent and so is the 'sarcasm' with which breaches of sociability are often presented in her narratives, the edge of which is turned in much the same direction as those ironies of juxtaposition employed by Fielding in the incident of the postillion in *Joseph Andrews*. That the passage on Mrs. Bennet's hospitality is far subtler and more insidious, in an almost *Tale of a Tub* manner, than Fielding's, is due to that advantage in such matters which some women once enjoyed over men. This advantage was clearly recognized by Francis, Lord Jeffrey:

> Their business being, as we have said, with actual or social life, and the colours it receives from the conduct and dispositions of individuals, they unconsciously acquire, at a very early age, the finest perception of character and manners, and are almost as soon instinctively schooled in the deep and more dangerous learning of feeling and emotions; while the very minuteness with which they make and mediate on these interesting observations, and the finer shades and variations of sentiment which are thus treasured and recorded, trains their whole faculties to a nicety and precision of operation, which often discloses itself to advantage in their application to studies of a different character.

The first part of Jeffrey's opening sentence, with all that it implies of female strength in the art of the novel, is worthy of general consideration. How far his remarks are true of women in general is a doubtful matter, but to read Jane Austen is to become aware of a fine 'perception of character and manners', of 'the finer variations of sentiment that are thus treasured and recorded' and of 'a nicety and precision of operation', all of which are particularized in the description of Mrs. Bennet's hospitality. Jeffrey himself goes on to consider the application of such a female intelligence to the art of the novel and, having mentioned works by several women authors, including Jane Austen, concludes,

> Those performances, too, are not only essentially and intensely feminine; but they are, in our judgment, decidedly more perfect than any masculine productions with which they can be brought into

comparison. They accomplish more completely all the ends at which they aim; and are worked out with a gracefulness and felicity of execution which excludes all idea of failure, and entirely satisfies the expectations they may have raised.

There could hardly be a finer judgement of Jane Austen than that offered here by one of her distinguished contemporaries. It needs only to be added that the gracefulness may be that of one who plays with a rapier and the felicity may be in choosing where precisely to insert it with a smile.

There is one further general point that needs to be made about the character of Jane Austen's writing, which is raised by Jeffrey's references to 'the deep and more dangerous learning of feeling and emotion' and 'the finer shades and variations of sentiment'. After the charges of sexual bias and narrow provincialism, the third common criticism likely to be levelled against Jane Austen's novels is that they are prissy. Love is never emotionally detailed and is touched upon only in passing – 'dearest, loveliest Elizabeth'. It might be remarked here that love is never emotionally detailed in *Wuthering Heights* either; it has no place in the novel's scheme of things and is abruptly dismissed by Cathy when the subject is raised by Nelly Dean. For both Jane Austen and Emily Brontë Love is a romantic abstraction and so of no particular relevance. However, for both of these novelists the lack of relevance is different from that imputed to it by Dr. Johnson. In Jane Austen's case the irresponsible infatuation of Lydia is not love; love is a matter not of transient passions but of lasting affections. For Jane Austen, affection for a parent, a brother, a sister and a husband is the same kind of affection, although in each case its mode of expression differs as do the attendant responsibilities and obligations. A century later, with passion rather than affection coming to be seen as the 'stuff' of love, we were all to be convicted by Freud of incestuous desires for our parents and kin. If passion is synonymous with love, then this is doubtless so, but in assuming that affection is the essence of love Jane Austen offers a much saner and more sociable view of it. She does not, it is nevertheless true, detail the intimacies of lovemaking; but then these are private activities which do not bear upon the primarily 'social' concerns of the novels: it is enough that we are told that Lydia is living with Wickham, in that it is enough that society knows this much.

In matters of sentiment and emotional tone Jane Austen's actual writing is far from prissy. Our first impression upon beginning to read *Pride and Prejudice* is

It is a truth universally acknowledged that a single man in possession of a good fortune must be in want of a wife.

There is no lack of emotional tone in this sarcastically Johnsonian utterance; a sarcasm at the expense of an opinion to which many readers seem to believe Jane Austen subscribes in the novels! The tone becomes more explicit as the narrative continues:

> However little known the feelings or views of such a man may be on first entering a neighbourhood, this truth is so well fixed in the minds of the surrounding families, that he is considered the rightful property of some one or other of their daughters.

Finally, in the concluding paragraph of the first brief chapter, the narrator's attitude to such matters is most plainly expressed in a biting description of Mrs. Bennet, chief representative in the novel of the presumptions so well hit off in the chapter:

> She was a woman of mean understanding, little information, and uncertain temper. When she was discontented, she fancied herself nervous. The business of her life was to get her daughters married; its solace was visiting and news.

This denigration of a life so narrowly circumscribed by the marrying-off of daughters, visiting and news should be a sufficient alert of the dangers of assuming that Jane Austen's novels are themselves concerned with nothing more.

The kind of female intelligence that Jane Austen brings to bear upon the world she anatomizes is irrepressible and tends to blur such distinctions as those between author, narrator and heroine. In *Pride and Prejudice* it links the style of the narrator with that of the heroine; the sarcasm of the narrator's opening declaration of 'a truth universally acknowledged' is echoed in Elizabeth's account of how she came to love Darcy:

> It has been coming on so gradually that I hardly know when it began; but I believe I must date it from my first seeing his beautiful grounds at Pemberley.

The same sarcastic manner, but here more caustic, is evident in Elizabeth's reply to Miss Bingley earlier in the novel:

'Your examination of Mr. Darcy is over, I presume,' said Miss Bingley; 'and pray what is the result?'

'I am perfectly convinced by it that Mr. Darcy has no defect. He owns it himself without disguise.'

The crisp, summary manner of the narrator ('She was a woman of mean understanding') is also characteristic of Elizabeth, as when she takes up arms for her sex against her sister Jane:

'Women fancy admiration means more than it does.'
'And men take care that they should.'

On such occasions Jane Austen, the narrator and the heroine appear to be as one.

The sarcastic and epigrammatic nature of Jane Austen's humour is quite evident and so too is its continual and serious implication. It is quite evident in the opening sentence of *Pride and Prejudice* and its relation to the brief paragraph which succeeds it. It is equally evident in Elizabeth's joke that she loved Darcy after seeing his grounds at Pemberley. What Elizabeth is ridiculing (and encouraging the reader to ridicule) is the idea that love bears any such relation to prosperity and property. It is a ridicule introduced in the first sentence and reiterated throughout the novel, tartly placing bourgeois marriage-brokering on a par with procuring. Before it is explicitly acknowledged by the narrator, the 'meanness' of Mrs. Bennet's 'understanding' is made evident when she exclaims of Bingley,

A single man of large fortune; four or five thousand a year. What a fine thing for our girls!

That in this Mrs. Bennet is merely the local and shameless representative of a general condition is established at the assembly or ball, where

Mr. Darcy soon drew the attention of the room by his fine, tall person, handsome features, noble mien, and the report . . . of his having ten thousand a year.

It is, however, Mrs. Bennet who (lacking the politeness needed to make her a socially acceptable, which is to say an accomplished, hypocrite) most clearly reveals the prostitutional nature of 'respectable' marriage. It is she who declares that

if a smart young colonel, with five or six thousand a year, should want
one of my girls, I shall not say nay to him

and who considers her eldest daughter's marriage

such a promising thing for her younger daughters, as Jane's marrying
so greatly must throw them in the way of other rich men . . .

The language – *want one of my girls, throw them in the way of . . . rich men* –
is that of a brothel-keeper.

In these instances the narrative attitude remains consistent with that of
the opening sentence of the novel and the authorial attitude, implicit in
the 'development' of Mrs. Bennet, with the initial pronouncement upon
the meanness of Mrs. Bennet's understanding. The attitude of the
narrator and that of the author are essentially the same, although the
author tends to be harsher than the narrator. Together they establish the
basic point of view of the novel and having done so proceed to
circumstantial complications of it, as in the narrator's observations upon
Wickham's pursuit of Mary King:

The sudden acquisition of ten thousand pounds was the most
remarkable charm of the young lady to whom he was now rendering
himself agreeable; but Elizabeth, less clear-sighted perhaps in this case
than in Charlotte's, did not quarrel with him for his wish of
independence. Nothing, on the contrary, could be more natural, and
while able to suppose that it cost him a few struggles to relinquish her,
she was ready to allow it a wise and desirable measure for both, and
could very sincerely wish him happy.

The ironic note is still present in that first sentence, qualifying Elizabeth's
reflection upon the propriety of Wickham's marrying to ensure his
financial independence. The liberality of Elizabeth's opinion of
Wickham's motives, in contrast to her opinion of Charlotte's desire to
marry for security, is further qualified by the suggestion that it is
dependent upon Elizabeth's being 'able to suppose that it cost' Wickham
'a few struggles to relinquish her'. In other words, the initial irony is
consolidated by the awareness that Elizabeth's judgement of Wickham's
behaviour is coloured by her vanity.

The incident itself does not qualify but rather substantiates the
narrator's well-established attitude. However, it does give rise to an

argument between Elizabeth and her aunt, Mrs. Gardiner, in which Elizabeth champions Wickham's behaviour in more general terms:

> Pray, my dear aunt, what is the difference in matrimonial affairs between the mercenary and the prudent motive? Where does discretion end and avarice begin? Last Christmas you were afraid of his marrying me, because it would be imprudent; and now, because he is trying to get a girl with only ten thousand pounds, you want to find out that he is mercenary.

It may seem that Elizabeth is equivocating and yet the distinction is crucial to the moral world of the novel. Lydia's elopement with Wickham is imprudent because Wickham is deeply in debt and has not the means to support wife. He has eloped with Lydia in a last desperate attempt to win some kind of income by marriage. His motive is transparently mercenary. On the other hand, Charlotte's marriage to Collins is eminently prudent.

> Without thinking highly either of men or of matrimony, marriage had always been her object: it was the only honourable provision for well-educated young women of small fortune, and, however uncertain of giving happiness, must be their pleasantest preservative from want.

There is little doubt that she will make Collins an admirable wife and although marriage to such a sycophant entails discomfort and embarrassment, which is only to be overcome by blunting her own sensibilities, Charlotte is plainly making the best of a bad job. Nevertheless, for both Charlotte and Collins the match is a sensible one under the social circumstances. Our disapproval differs from Elizabeth's, being directed by the novel against a society in which marriage is the 'pleasantest preservative from want' of well-educated young women of small fortune.

Jane Austen, then, avoids the nonsense of pretending that money doesn't matter: the mercenary motive is subject to sarcasm; the prudent motive, though (as in Charlotte's case) felt to be pathetic, is treated with sympathy: the ideal arrangement is one in which (as in Elizabeth's and Darcy's case) real affection is affluently rewarded.

Much that has been said of the concern for income in *Pride and Prejudice* holds true for its concern for status. Sir William, it will be remembered, is gently ridiculed for his preoccupation with his suddenly acquired rank. In Chapter 10, the narrator informs us that 'Darcy had never been so bewitched by any woman' as he was by Elizabeth and that 'He really believed that, were it not for the inferiority of her connections, he should be in some danger'. That this is a reflection of Darcy's characteristic fault, false pride, is made apparent as the novel proceeds and the general attitude towards this is finally made quite explicit in Chapter 33. Elizabeth has been informed by Colonel Fitzwilliam that there are strong objections to Bingley's marriage to Jane and the narrator comments,

> these strong objections probably were her having one uncle who was a country attorney, and another who was in business in London.

The narrative account of Elizabeth's reaction to this possibility is that Darcy, in breaking-up the association between Bingley and Jane, 'had been partly governed by the worst kind of pride'. Whether or not this is considered fair comment on Darcy's reasons does not affect the characterization of a concern for social status as 'the worst kind of pride'. Much the same point is made by Elizabeth in conversation with her aunt. What is in question is the possibility of Bingley visiting Jane whilst Jane is staying at her aunt's house in Gracechurch Street.

> Mr. Darcy may, perhaps, have *heard* of such a place as Gracechurch Street, but he would hardly think a month's ablution enough to cleanse him from its impurities, were he once to enter it . . .

Again, whether the comment does justice to Darcy is irrelevant; what is relevant is the felt justness of the judgement of anyone who has such a sense of the importance of social status.

Throughout the novel the snobbery of status is treated with varied disapproval, obliquely in the idiocy of Collins –

> Lady Catherine herself says that, in point of true beauty, Miss De Burgh is far superior to the handsomest of her sex; because there is that in her features which marks the young woman of distinguished birth.

– and directly in the scathing retort of Elizabeth after Miss Bingley has concluded her exposure of Wickham's character:

'I pity you, Miss Eliza, for this discovery of your favourite's guilt; but really, considering his descent, one could not expect much better.'

'His guilt and his descent appear, by your account, to be the same,' said Elizabeth angrily; 'for I have heard you accuse him of nothing worse than of being the son of Mr. Darcy's steward. . . .'

Alternatively there is the sympathetic characterization of the Gardiners, tradespeople who stand in sharp contrast to the initial snobbery of Darcy, the Bingley sisters, Lady Catherine, and the inane monomania of Mrs. Bennet. The novel persistently and consistently pillories what the narrator refers to as 'the stateliness of money and rank'.

Wealth and social status are not as distinct in *Pride and Prejudice* as the foregoing exegesis may have suggested: those who have rank usually have wealth and those who have wealth commonly have rank. Nor is the matter of wealth and rank distinct from that of the relationship of the sexes. Darcy is protected from the bewitching Elizabeth by an awareness of 'the inferiority of her connections'. Pathetically, Charlotte's marriage to Collins is excused by the observation that for women in Charlotte's position marriage is the 'pleasantest preservative from want'. Set against these constrained and negative attitudes towards the relations between the sexes there are certain positive affirmations. Such is Elizabeth's declaration to her aunt, who fears that her niece is becoming entangled with Wickham:

since we see, every day, that where there is affection young people are seldom withheld, by immediate want of fortune, from entering into engagements with each other, how can I promise to be wiser than so many of my fellow creatures, if I am tempted? or how am I even to know that is would be wisdom to resist? All that I can promise you, therefore, is not to be in a hurry.

That is balanced and sane, it does not hide from the facts of life nor does it merely succumb to them. It may be wise to give way to the affections, but it can never be wise to do so blindly. The implicit counsel is one of prudence; lack of consideration is the real danger and not a fortuneless marriage.

Prudence, due consideration, especially for the feelings of others, occupies a central place in the moral scheme of Jane Austen's novels. It is one of those standards of integrity to which Elizabeth appeals in exposing to the reader something of the moral weakness of the angelic Jane:

My dear Jane, Mr. Collins is a conceited, pompous, narrow-minded, silly man: you know he is, as well as I do; and you must feel, as well as I do, that the woman who marries him cannot have a proper way of thinking. You shall not defend her, though it is Charlotte Lucas. You shall not, for the sake of one individual, change the meaning of principle and integrity, not endeavour to persuade yourself or me that selfishness is prudence, and insensibility of danger security for happiness.

However ill-judged Charlotte's situation is here, there is no suggestion anywhere that the appeal to prudence is irrelevant or that Elizabeth is wrong to define insensibility, a lack of consideration, as revealing a lack of principle and integrity. Elizabeth drives hom the point a few lines later:

'I am far from attributing any part of Mr. Bingley's conduct to design,' said Elizabeth; 'but without scheming to do wrong or to make others unhappy, there may be error and there may be misery. Thoughtlessness, want of attention to other people's feelings, and want of resolution will do the business.'

It is because thoughtfulness and consideration, prudence, are so central to the humanity of the novel that so much emphasis is placed in it upon education. One of the distinctions drawn between Mr. Gardiner and his sister, Mrs. Bennet, is that he is greatly superior to her in education. It is presumed that someone who has received a good education will be more capable of thoughtfulness and consideration than someone who has not; doubtless that is the measure of a good education.

Consideration involves, in Elizabeth's words, 'attention to other people's feelings' and is felt to be a matter of principle, integrity and good sense. The narrator reflects upon Jane's feelings for Bingley

that all her good sense, and all her attention to the feelings of her friends, were requisite to check the indulgence of those regrets which must have been injurious to her own health and their tranquillity.

'Good sense' and 'attention to the feelings of her friends' (or, more generally, 'attention to other people's feelings') reveal the standards against which the judgements of the novel are made, whether explicitly or implicitly, in the irony of tone and situation. About what too commonly passes for moral comment the novel is as scathingly sarcastic as it is about social snobbery and mercenary-mindedness. Thus, in Chapter 12, Jane and Elizabeth find

> Mary, as usual, deep in the study of thorough bass and human nature; and had some new extracts to admire, and some new observations of threadbare morality to listen to.

An instance of such an observation is provided in Mary's response to Lydia's plight:

> Unhappy as the event must be for Lydia, we may draw from it this useful lesson: that loss of virtue in a female is irretrievable, that one false step involves her in endless ruin, that her reputation is no less brittle than it is beautiful, and that she cannot be too much guarded in her behaviour towards the undeserving of the other sex.

The proper response to such hard-hearted piety is enacted for the reader by Elizabeth:

> Elizabeth lifted up her eyes in amazement, but was too much oppressed to make any reply. Mary, however, continued to console herself with such kind of moral extractions from the evil before them.

Conventional, hard-hearted piety is also sardonically caricatured in Collins' letter of condolence upon the elopement of Lydia, in which Collins 'consoles' Mrs. Bennet with the thought that 'The death of your daughter would have been a blessing in comparison of this.' The letter continues in the same heartlessly lunatic vein.

Income, status, sex and morals are concerns which run through *Pride and Prejudice* like interweaving threads, knitting together the social fabric of the novel. They are not the only threads, but they are prominent ones, receiving emphasis and commanding attention. However, it is not the emphasis and attention bestowed upon them but the nature of the emphasis and the kind of attention this defines that is of primary importance. When these last are considered we find a sensible and intelligent as well as a warmly human attitude informing the novel.

Jane Austen's subject matter was not chosen at random and it would be quite wrong to say that it is only the attitudes of her prose that are of importance and that the matter upon which they play is fortuitous. It is

evident from the very title *Pride and Prejudice*, however, that the novel is
primarily concerned with attitudes and dispositions and the novel itself
confirms that it is not events but reactions to events that are of central
importance. This is essential to the purport of the novel: upon how slight
an initial foundation is Elizabeth's complex of reactions to Darcy reared;
at what slight straws does the angelic Jane clutch in order to exercise her
goodness in trying to excuse fools and knaves their folly and villainy.
The pattern of their behaviour here is to be found in Mrs. Bennet, whose
reactions to events are out of all sensible proportion to the importance of
the events themselves; truly both Jane and Elizabeth are their mother's
daughters. Jane Austen's concern for sanity is what lies behind and is
expressed in this concentration upon the reaction rather than the event.

Whilst the novel is a novel of attitudes, amongst the most dominant of
which are those to income, rank and the relations of the sexes, the central
area of its subject matter reveals the foundations of its attitudes and
judgements. The core of the novel is the study of the Bennet family: the
sarcastic irresponsibility of Mr. Bennet, the over-charitableness of Jane,
the aggressive and witty commonsense of Elizabeth, the flightiness of
Lydia, the harsh and insensitive moralising of Mary. Upon this highly
volatile little world impinges the bluff good-nature of Bingley, the
enigmatic aloofness of Darcy, the spitefulness of the Bingley sisters, the
smooth cunning of Collins, the self-opinionated hauteur of Lady
Catherine de Burgh and the affectionate kindliness of the Gardiners.

Our first acquaintance with the Bennets occurs in the opening chapter,
but it is not until much later in the novel that the narrator, in considering
Elizabeth's opinion of marriage, analyses the Bennet family in closer
detail.

Had Elizabeth's opinion been all drawn from her own family, she
could not have formed a very pleasing picture of conjugal felicity or
domestic comfort. Her father, captivated by youth and beauty, and
that appearance of good humour which youth and beauty generally
give, had married a woman whose weak understanding and illiberal
mind had very early in their marriage put an end to all real affection
for her. Respect, esteem, and confidence had vanished for ever; and all
his views of domestic happiness were overthrown. But Mr. Bennet
was not of a disposition to seek comfort for the disappointment which
his own imprudence had brought on in any of those pleasures which so
often console the unfortunate for their folly or their vice. He was fond
of the country and of books; and from these tastes had arisen his

principal enjoyments. To his wife he was very little otherwise indebted then as her ignorance and folly had contributed to his amusement. This is not the sort of happiness which a man would in general wish to owe to his wife; but where other powers of entertainment are wanting, the true philosopher will derive benefit from such as are given.

Elizabeth, however, had never been blind to the impropriety of her father's behaviour as a husband. She had always seen it with pain; but respecting his abilities, and grateful for his affectionate treatment of herself, she endeavoured to forget what she could not overlook, and to banish from her thoughts that continual breach of conjugal obligation and decorum which, in exposing his wife to the contempt of her own children, was so highly reprehensible. But she had never felt so strongly as now the disadvantages which must attend the children of so unsuitable a marriage, nor ever been so fully aware of the evils arising from so ill-judged a direction of talents – talents which, rightly used, might at least have preserved the respectability of his daughters, even if incapable of enlarging the mind of his wife.

The little network of relationships at the centre of the novel, the Bennet family, are badly, indeed it seems irreparably, flawed and the flaw is the result of an imprudent marriage. The analysis provided by the narrator here justifies the great care and attention devoted to courtship and marriage throughout the novel. It also gives additional significance to other aspects of the novel. Darcy, for instance, is proud and his pride prevents him from seeking a romantic alliance with Elizabeth. Darcy's pride here may be construed as social snobbery; Elizabeth's family are not high enough in the social scale for Darcy to contemplate marriage to her. At this level the concerns of the novel are being understood as overtly social. Darcy's pride, however, may also be seen as moral snobbery; the condition of the Bennet family (as outlined by the narrator) – the stupidities of the mother, the flightiness of the sister, the irresponsibility of the father – appears obnoxious to Darcy's sense of fitness. On this view, the novel is essentially moral. Quite obviously, the novel is neither exclusively moral nor exclusively social; at times the social consideration is to the fore and at others the moral one. The ambivalence itself is what is truly remarkable.

Earlier, reference was made to the brief biographies of Sir William Lucas and the Bingley sisters to illustrate Jane Austen's use of the shifting implication. The ambiguities involved there represent a common feature of her prose style. In both those instances and in many others like them throughout the novel, the irony of the narrative proceeds by way of a surreptitious movement back and forth between the moral and the social appraisal of the attitudes and behaviour of such as Sir William Lucas and the Bingley sisters. This movement is maintained throughout the novel and the ambiguity, referred to in connection with Darcy's pride, is a mode of procedure in the novel and a major element of its style; it is an irreducible fact of Jane Austen's manner.

The importance of this element of style is obvious; it ensures that the critical viewpoint of the narrative is never surrendered to the moral standards of the life under consideration; those standards are subject to political appraisal. Thus, for instance, in the passage on the Bingley sisters, their social circumstances are said to give them a right to think meanly of others; the irony of the passage is due to the shift from social to moral appraisal and it is a shift most carefully achieved. The machinery of it is provided by the very structure of the passage — social circumstances . . . which bestow a right . . . which justifies them in thinking meanly of others. The circumstances are social but the justification is of a moral attitude and consequently the right asserted is ambiguous; it is social in that it refers back to social circumstances and moral in that it refers forward to the moral attitude. Part of the difficulty in nailing down the irony of this particular passage is due to the fact that it lies in the ambiguity of *right*, an ambiguity that is unlikely to be remarked upon reading the passage. This social-moral ambiguity of *right* is a local instance of that more general ambiguity represented in Darcy's pride.

So, having perceived that the condition of the Bennet family is a badly flawed one, we begin to recognize that Darcy's pride in not wishing to ally himself with such a family is a two-faced thing, it is a social pride, a pride of rank, and it is a moral pride, the pride of a man with moral sensibilities in the face of those who fail to measure up to his own standards. Now this is not to say that there is a sense, namely a moral sense, in which the pride of Darcy is treated as a positive virtue. On the contrary, the obvious flaws of the Bennet family find their complement in those of Darcy, just as the ingratiating behaviour of Mrs. Bennet has as its complement the aloofness and condescension of Darcy's behaviour. To put the matter in a didactic way, one could say that Darcy has to learn humility; he has to learn to humble his pride, both his moral pride and his pride of social place and rank. He has, as it were, to come from behind his façade of place and propriety and enter into a more intimate and direct relationship with those about him. The inadequacies of these twin façades, rank and moral propriety, are strikingly revealed in the characterization of, say, Mary and Lady Catherine de Burgh. It is as though, in such characters as these, Jane Austen has drawn a clear distinction between the two sides of the ambiguity of her interest, and has simultaneously driven home the stupidities of moral and social pride. The threadbare morality of Mary and the snobbery of Lady Catherine de Burgh are, one might say, merely exaggerations of the initial condition of Darcy; it is this condition he has to grow out of, he has to learn humility and he has to learn sympathy. I say 'he has to' not because this is a condition of his future happiness or something of that sort, but because of his function in revealing the purpose of the novel. It is not really a case of his having to do anything but of his actually doing something; not that he has to develop in this way but that he does develop in this way.

The fact of Darcy's development is something to consider in judging what the novel, *Pride and Prejudice*, is about. Darcy is brought to realize that the moral and social sensibilities which he represents, and which express a certain standard of aristocratic breeding and manner, are lacking in the fitness he initially believes them to possess and which Lady Catherine de Burgh and Mr. Collins continue to believe them to possess. In place of such sensibilities there are developed, in the development of Darcy's character, wider and more democratic sympathies. For Jane Austen's genius is essentially sociable and in *Pride and Prejudice*, as in her other novels, the division of society into classes is realized to create barriers to the flow of human sympathy and understanding, barriers only to be overcome by considerable and sustained effort. Much of Darcy's initial pride is the pride felt to be characteristic of his class, something he shares with the only other aristocrat in the novel, Lady Catherine. So too, much of the prejudice that shapes Elizabeth's initial reaction to him is that of (what the Vicar of Wakefield calls) the 'middle order of mankind' in the face of the condescending aristocrat. Society being what it is in the world of Jane Austen, these are the barriers that transform fellow feeling into the feeling of one class for another; but, if these are the barriers which separate, what are the ties that bind? Jane Austen's attempt to answer that question distinguishes her art quite clearly from that of Swift and some understanding of her answer is most crucially involved in the appreciation of *Persuasion*.

(2)

There is no English novelist who can express society through character and dialogue as well as Jane Austen. We might compare *Persuasion* in this respect with *Middlemarch* as represented by some critics. George Eliot, on the critical view I have in mind, is plainly incapable of actualizing *Middlemarch* itself through character and dialogue: it is the unrelenting and unalterable mechanism in the aspiring body of the novel; it shatters and defeats the aspirations that seek to effect an alteration in it; its only expression is in the destruction of whatever ideals enter into the characterization of the novel. Consequently, Kettle has seen in the novel a perfidious dualism between society and the aggregate of characters. Whatever one's view of this opinion of *Middlemarch*, it is plain that it could not be held of *Persuasion*. The society or, as Jeffrey quite properly calls it, the actual life of the novel is self-evidently more variegated than that ascribed to *Middlemarch*; it is, as it were, the resolution of all those forces which are communicated to us in dialogue and characterization. Consider, for example, the characterization of Lady Russell:

> She was a woman rather of sound than of quick abilities, whose difficulties in coming to any decision in this instance were great, from the opposition of two leading principles. She was of strict integrity herself, with a delicate sense of honour; but she was desirous of saving Sir Walter's feelings, as solicitous for the credit of the family, as aristocratic in her ideas of what was due to them, as anybody of sense and honesty could well be. She was a benevolent, charitable, good woman, and capable of strong attachments, most correct in her conduct, strict in her motions of decorum and with manners that were held a standard of good breeding. She had a cultivated mind, and was, generally speaking, rational and consistent; but she had prejudices on the side of ancestry; she had a value for rank and consequence, which blinded her a little to the faults of those who possessed them.

The social and individual valuations of character here are inseparable: Lady Russell's sense of honour and her aristocratic ideas are expressed in her valuation of family, just as her weaknesses are realized in her appraisal of social standing. The narrator, incidentally, is characteristically detached from the social evaluations, representing both their strength and their weakness. For the narrator, as will later appear, it is not the level but the quality of social life that is of significance.

It is obvious enough that the qualities of social life expressed in Elizabeth and Sir Walter are compounded of pride, vanity, self-importance, all terms used in the novel to describe them and to create a sense of a pretentious world inhabited by hollow creatures. Their existence is just such a 'nothingness' as Lawrence writes of in describing certain qualities of life in *Lady Chatterley's Lover*: it is a term used in characterizing the life of Elizabeth Elliot:

> Such were Elizabeth Elliot's sentiments and sensations; such the cares to alloy, the agitations to vary, the sameness and the elegance, the prosperity and the nothingness of her scene of life; such the feelings to give interest to a long, uneventful residence in one country circle, to fill the vacancies which there were no habits of utility abroad, no talents or accomplishments for home, to occupy.

The valuations are still social; they are centred upon Home, Abroad, the Country Circle, upon life clearly defined in social terms. And one turns from this paucity, this empty round, to the life of the Harville household at Lyme, which provides the criterion against which are measured the circles of life described by the novel.

The Harvilles themselves are the essential criterion:

> Captain Harville . . . was a perfect gentleman, unaffected, warm and obliging. Mrs. Harville, a degree less polished than her husband, seemed, however, to have the same good feelings . . .

They are 'kindly, hospitable',

> in a degree of hospitality so uncommon, so unlike the usual style of give-and-take invitations, and dinners of formality and display . . .

Theirs, we are told, is the hospitality of 'those who invite from the heart'. Their cottage is as much a part of their characterization as the mirrors in Sir Walter's bedroom are of his. The cottage is decorated with the fruits of Captain Harville's labours, both with things gathered in his profession and things actually produced by himself:

> His lameness prevented him from taking much exercise; but a mind of usefulness and ingenuity seemed to furnish him with constant

employment within. He drew, he varnished, he carpentered, he glued; he made toys for the children; he fashioned new netting needles and pins with improvements; and if everything else was done, sat down to his large fishing net at one corner of the room.

We are coming to some understanding of the kind of qualities which are to be thought of as characterizing a useful and valuable social existence. It is worth itemizing these to suggest the presumptions from which the novel's judgements proceed. Domesticity is one; that honest or unpretentious and affectionate family existence epitomized by the Harvilles. Hospitality is another (this has already been remarked in the characterization of the Harvilles and it may also be remarked in that of Mrs. Musgrove). We are not as sharply aware, perhaps, of the positive value of hospitality as our ancestors were or as other nations still are; this may be one of the reasons why we cannot fully respond to the heinousness of Macbeth's crime, even though Macbeth himself stresses that the breach in the natural order of things which is effected by the murder of Duncan is a breach of hospitality. The family and hospitality come as high in Jane Austen's scheme of things as they do in Shakespeare's. The concern for hospitality, evident in the characterization of the Harvilles, is also, though very differently, evident in the characterization of Elizabeth:

Elizabeth was, for a short time, suffering a good deal. She felt that Mrs. Musgrove and all her party ought to be asked to dine with them; but she could not bear to have the difference of style, the reduction of servants, which a dinner must betray, witnessed by those who had been always so inferior to the Elliots of Kellynch. It was a struggle between propriety and vanity; but vanity got the better, and then Elizabeth was happy again.

In this Elizabeth's behaviour may be compared with that which the Harvilles' visitors met from 'their new friends':

they all went in-doors with their new friends and found rooms so small as none but those who invite from the heart could think capable of accommodating so many.

The point makes itself in the comparison: hospitality is the second of those values which direct the judgements present in the novel. The third

is warmth and real affection. This is omnipresent in Jane Austen's novels.
It may be a counsel of prudence that men and women should not marry
without sufficient fortune or a similarity of breeding, but such
considerations are suspended whenever real affection enters into the
match. Perhaps the positive values which direct *Persuasion* can be
summed-up in the testimony to Mr. Elliot:

> Everything united in him; good understanding, correct opinions,
> knowledge of the world, and a warm heart. He had strong feelings of
> family attachment and family honour, without pride or weakness; he
> lived with the liberality of a man of fortune, without display; he
> judged for himself in everything essential, without defying public
> opinion in any point of wordly decorum. He was steady, observant,
> moderate, candid, never run away with by spirits or by selfishness,
> which fancied itself strong feeling: and yet, with a sensibility to what
> was amiable and lovely, and a value for all the felicities of domestic
> life, which characters of fancied enthusiasm and violent agitation
> seldom really possess.

That it later transpires that Mr. Elliot does not deserve such a reference
does not diminish its testimony to the standards of behaviour which
inform the novel.

Nowadays many of the qualities for which Mr. Elliot is commended
may seem of doubtful worth, for a modern reader may be slow to
appreciate the kinds of judgement implicit in several of Jane Austen's key
terms. Propriety, for instance, is not a concern for form, as witness the
passage on Elizabeth quoted above, where the concern for form, for
keeping up appearances, is *vanity* whilst a proper hospitality is referred to
as *propriety*. Similarly, care needs to be taken in understanding such terms
as 'correct opinions' and 'worldly decorum' in the glowing reference
afforded Mr. Elliot; these are terms associated with that quite central
term 'manners'. The best way of describing what Jane Austen means
by 'manners' is to say that she uses the word to describe behaviour
which is motivated by a complete regard for the feelings of others;
under no circumstances should behaviour be such as to cause discomfort to others no matter what one's personal feelings about them
may be. Hence Elliot is commended because he was 'never run away
with by spirits or by selfishness, which fancied itself strong feeling'.
Hence also, of course, the care expected in conduct between the sexes:
Wentworth's behaviour is wrong because it is likely to give rise to

feelings in Louise Musgrove which Wentworth does not intend to satisfy.

It is because manners express a concern for feelings that they are so consistently linked with good breeding and education, as when Elliot remarks,

'Good company requires only birth, education, and manners, and with regard to education is not very nice. Birth and good manners are essential; but a little learning is by no means a dangerous thing in good company; on the contrary, it will do very well. My cousin Anne shakes her head. She is not satisfied. She is fastidious.'

In this Jane Austen is, as in most things, also fastidious. Education is felt to be important because it permits the kind of fine discrimination in matters of feeling and judgement upon which good manners are based. Good manners, however, though central to the judgements of the novel, are not essential; they are the means by which self-concern is rendered subservient to a concern for the feelings of others and where we meet with natural magnanimity – as in the case of Mrs. Harville and Admiral and Mrs. Croft – they are unnecessary. As a code of behaviour, manners are a second best, a means of remedying natural deficiencies; it is a code to which Mrs. Smith did not have to apply, for

here was that elasticity of mind, that disposition to be comforted, that power of turning readily from evil to good, and of finding employment which carried her out of herself, which was from nature alone. It was the choicest gift of Heaven. . . .

In less naturally gifted characters, manners supply the want of that power of being carried out of the self. The hypocrisy, pride and vanity of Sir Walter and Elizabeth arise entirely from concern for self at the expense not only of Anne but of everyone and everything with which they come into contact, even their very good friend Mrs. Clay is esteemed their very good friend because she panders to their self-concern. Theirs is the height of bad manners.

Family, Propriety, Decorum, Opinion, Manners; these are the observances of a compact human world, a community small enough to remain personal, guided in its social behaviour by a concern for personal relations and controlling individual feelings in the communal interest.

The world of the novel is made up of a number of such communities. When Anne goes to Uppercross, she is aware that she is going to a community which is different from that at Kellynch:

> Anne had not wanted this visit to Uppercross to learn that a removal from one set of people to another, though at a distance of only three miles, will often include a total change of conversation, opinion, and idea. She had never been staying there before, without being struck by it, or without wishing that other Elliots would have her advantage in seeing how unknown, or unconsidered there, were the affairs which at Kellynch Hall were treated as of such general publicity and pervading interest; yet, with all this experience, she believed she must now submit to feel another lesson, in the art of knowing our own nothingness beyond our own circle, was become necessary to her . . .

At Uppercross, therefore, Anne is not merely at another house, amidst another family, of the same social background and sharing the same social ethos as the Elliots, she is, in a sense the novel makes apparent, in another realm:

> She acknowledged it to be very fitting, that every little social commonwealth should dictate its own matters of discourse; and hoped, ere long, to become a not unworthy member of the one she was now transplanted into. With the prospect of spending at least two months at Uppercross, it was highly incumbent on her to clothe her imagination, her memory, and all her ideas in as much of Uppercross as possible.

In *Persuasion* there are three such social commonwealths: Kellynch Hall, Uppercross and the Harvilles' at Lyme. In the novel Jane Austen, in exploring these, is separating and analysing the constituents of a larger whole, before bringing them together to constitute one society, one complex interweaving of these little worlds, at Bath. Here, finally, the area of life is extended, the judgement (as of the Elliots) is socially more comprehensive, stretching from the nobility, the Dalrymples, to the impoverished Mrs. Smith. Here the novel's judgements assume a sharper political edge, as Sir Walter and Elizabeth are placed by their connection with the Dalrymples and Mr. Elliot by the poverty of Mrs. Smith.

Hopefully, sufficient has been said to give a general impression of *Persuasion*'s concern 'with actual or social life'. Just as a poet such as

Wyatt sets out to explore the human qualities of the social complex with which he was most intimate, that of the Court, so does Jane Austen in the case of the gentry. It is perhaps pertinent to remark that in both of these instances the social complex in question, the Court and the gentry, produces its anatomist at a moment just prior to its extinction as a powerful directive force in English life. Both Jane Austen and Wyatt (in this they may be compared with Balzac) lack that over-riding confidence in the society *to which they belong* for their work to act as a vigorous expression of its way of life and, indeed, their work is highly self-conscious and critical of it. But they *do* still belong to the way of life upon which they reflect so critically. Their standards are still those of the Court, on the one hand, and those of the gentry on the other. Consequently, their work *in toto* expresses a crisis; initially a crisis of consciousness, more generally a crisis in a way of life, a way of acting and evaluating, a way of living together. Both come to measure the present actualities of their respective ways of life according to ideals that are actually, really, denied; and both seek, as it were, to repair reality by affirming in their art the victory of old ideals over present realities. Neither artist is content with this solution and, to some extent, both are critical of it as a solution. Consequently in Jane Austen one has levels of critical consciousness and judgement; there is not only a self-conscious judgement of a generally accepted way of living, there is also a hyper-conscious judgement of that judgement. To put it in terms which bring it closer to *Persuasion*, there is the persuasive attempt to realize the positive values of a way of life that suffers from actual flaws – flaws of family pride, pride of rank, pride of opinion – and there is also the wider and more profound judgement of this persuasion.

The code which we are persuaded to accept in high seriousness as an expression of a valuable way of living, and which has already been referred to as 'good manners', is constantly invoked as the criterion against which those first-level judgements in the novel are made. It is invoked in the early approbation of Mr. Elliot – his present behaviour conforms to the code; it is the code which was invoked by Lady Russell in persuading Anne to reject Wentworth's first proposal. It is equally plain that although these judgements may come to appear as wrong, nevertheless the standard applied was the right one; the whole weight of Jane Austen's initial commitment lies behind that standard, that code of manners. This persuasion to accept the code as a valuable criterion, however, is itself being treated critically by Jane Austen. It is seen, and seen clearly, as a code of social behaviour, a code governing appearances, and its limitations arise from the fact that appearances can often mislead – as in Mr. Elliot's case. Here we encounter that level of hyper-consciousness mentioned above.

Consider how this affects the art of judgement in *Persuasion*. Earlier I referred to the inadequacies and obvious follies of Sir Walter and Elizabeth in relation to the criteria provided by the code of manners – they are inhospitable, pushing, etc. This is the judgement supported by the first-level appraisal. To feel that this is an adequate judgement is to feel the full force of Jane Austen's commitment to the code of manners, to the ideals of the social complex she anatomizes. And at this level we appreciate the sense of family connection (not connection of rank, just of family) which is so positively expressed in Anne; at this level we agree with Mrs. Smith when she asserts that 'Even the smooth surface of a family union seems worth preserving though there may be nothing durable beneath.' This acceptance is at the level of subscription to the code of manners, at the self-conscious level on which the first judgements of the novel are made. But there is also that hyper-conscious judgement of the novel; one which is at work assessing the code of manners itself, or more particularly the world of appearances which the code controls, a judgement which prompts such awareness as that of the 'elegant stupidity of private parties', of the narrow round, the trifling heart, of the fact that 'When one lives in the world, a man or woman's marrying for money is too common to strike one as it ought.' It is this judgement which commands explicit attention and controls our retrospective assessment of the novel as we read the final pages. Thus, for instance, Lady Russell,

> must learn to feel that she had been mistaken with regard to both [Mr. Elliot and Wentworth]; that she had been unfairly influenced by appearances in each; that because Captain Wentworth's manners had not suited her own ideas, she had been too quick in suspecting them to indicate a character of dangerous impetuosity; and that because Mr. Elliot's manners had precisely pleased her in their propriety and correctness, their general politness and suavity, she had been too quick in receiving them as the certain result of the most correct opinions and well-regulated mind.

It is not possible to resist the opportunity to comment at this point that this placing of Lady Russell is a placing of 'propriety' and 'correctness' of 'manners' as adequate means of judgement; they are not irrelevant, but they are certainly not adequate and in themselves are not to be relied upon.

Perhaps the best way of briefly summing up the awareness behind the complex and two-tiered evaluation pressed for in the novel is to say that it is an awareness that, in social or actual life, a code of manners (of behaviour) is necessary but not sufficient. We are reacting too crudely to the complexities of actual living if we see the matter as one of the value of the forms of social behaviour versus the values of spontaneous life – that warmth and affection so frequently and pointedly appealed to in the work of Jane Austen. There is one particular in the novel in which it is essential to appreciate the relationship between correct forms of social behaviour and the demands of spontaneous affection, and that is, of course, in appreciating the influence exerted by Lady Russell in persuading Anne to break off her engagement to Wentworth. To understand the nature of Lady Russell's influence, the reader must recognize the capacity in which she exercises it. I have already quoted a passage from the end of the novel in which Anne is represented as reflecting upon the limited awareness of Lady Russell; in a dialogue between Anne and Wentworth at the end of the penultimate chapter we find a definition of the proper relationship between this limited awareness and, what may be called, the social forms, correct behaviour.

'I have been thinking over the past [says Anne to Wentworth] and trying impartially to judge of the right and wrong, I mean with regard to myself; and I must believe that I was right, much as I suffered from it, that I was perfectly right in being guided by the friend whom you will love better than you do now. *To me, she was in the place of a parent.* Do not mistake me, however. I am not saying that she did not err in her advice. It was, perhaps, one of those cases in which advice is good or bad only as the event decides; and for myself, I certainly never should, in any circumstance of tolerable similarity, give such advice. But I mean, that I was right in submitting to her, and that if I had done otherwise, I should have suffered more in continuing the engagement than I did even in giving it up, because I should have suffered in my conscience. I have now, as far as such a settlement is allowable in human nature, nothing to reproach myself with; and if I mistake not, a strong sense of duty is no bad part of a woman's portion.' (My italics.)

Was Anne right to submit to advice that later proved wrong and which even at the time went against the inclination of her affections? Yes, is the answer we are given. But can we accept it? Here we broach a matter that is no mere literary one. The importance of the family in Jane Austen's scheme of things, in her social valuations, has already been remarked, and it is to this that we are referred here: 'To me, she was in the place of a parent.' It is this acceptance of family duty – of family piety, if you like – that underwrites the propriety and correctness of Anne's submission to the advice of Lady Russell. Here, then, is a good illustration of an order of values in which family-like affection and respect – and consequently a sense of duty – is seen as taking proper preference over other kinds of affection and duty. There is never any suggestion that Anne has been wrongly persuaded by Lady Russell; it is essential to see this in order to give proper weight to that interest in persuasion which led Jane Austen to choose the word for her title. The family, that little social commonwealth, should come first – that is the judgement we arrive at and that is the judgement upon which Anne acts in breaking off her engagement. Anne is persuaded, but she is rightly persuaded, and the rightness lies in that evaluation of the importance of familial ties and obligations.

How important these connections are felt to be is made plain enough to the reader at the end of the novel, as Anne reflects that she

> had no other alloy to the happiness of her prospects than what arose from the consciousness of having no relations to bestow on him [Wentworth] which a man of sense could value. There she felt her own inferiority keenly. The disproportion in their fortune was nothing; it did not give her a moment's regret; but to have no family to receive and estimate him properly, nothing of respectability, of harmony, of good will, to offer in return for all the worth and all the prompt welcome which met her in his brothers and sisters, was a source of as lively pain as her mind could well be sensible of under circumstances of otherwise strong felicity. She had but two friends in the world to add to his list, Lady Russell and Mrs. Smith.

Again it seems opportune to call attention to the use of a word, the word 'respectability': Anne had 'nothing of respectability' to offer Wentworth. This, it hardly needs remarking, is not the respectability of appearances, of rank and place – her father and sisters had this – it is respectability in the sense of 'respectworthy'. Its ambiguity is implicitly questioning: are the conventionally respectable (i.e. those who are conventionally respected) really respectable (i.e. worthy of respect)? As

Jane Austen explores the cracks which open up in society when such discriminations are made there emerges a new and more intense concern for 'manners', not as the forms of behaviour practised or professed by the gentry, but as a mediation between individual and social life, between regulation and spontaneity, between what Jane Austen describes in the title of another novel as 'sense and sensibility'.

It has become difficult for us nowadays to place any authority above that of our own feelings; to give the supremacy to some external regulation such as family piety. Yet it is plainly this sense of some necessary, over-riding authority which creates the hyper-consciousness in *Persuasion*, just as it is the acceptance of the code of manners which informs its self-consciousness. We must, the point is, observe good manners, but we must also be aware that good manners are simply means of giving social expression to certain values and this requires a double judgement – are these good manners? and do such good manners serve to express such values as those of family piety? And it is in terms of this double judgement that the novels proceed. Whether we can or cannot accept the specific values honoured by Jane Austen, we can perceive the intelligence which can simultaneously relate social and individual valuations and assess the quality of human living as it actually exists – that is to say, as an interdependence of individual and society – and not as it exists in thinking, in which society is one abstraction and the individual is another.

But, I suppose, when we think of *Persuasion* we think more frequently not of the central persuasions which are preoccupying the novel – the persuasive power of the code of manners as expressed in Mr. Elliot or the persuasive power of spontaneous feeling as expressed in Lady Russell – what we tend to think of are those particularly comic passages of overt persuasion such as characterize, above all, the less respectable members of the Elliot family – Sir Walter, Elizabeth and Mary. The kind of thing we have directly in mind is well represented by the complaints pressed upon Anne by Mary and the Musgroves in Chapter VI.

One of the least agreeable circumstances of her residence there, was her being treated with too much confidence by all parties, and being too much in the secret of the complaints of each house. Known to have some influence with her sister, she was continually requested, or at least receiving hints to exert it, beyond what was practicable. 'I wish you could persuade Mary not to be always fancying herself ill,' was Charles's language; and in an unhappy mood, thus spoke Mary: – 'I do believe if Charles were to see me dying, he would not think there was any thing the matter with me. I am sure, Anne, if you would, you might persuade him that I really am very ill – a great deal worse than I ever own.'

Mary's declaration was, 'I hate sending the children to the Great House, though their grandmamma is always wanting to see them, for she humours and indulges them to such a degree, and gives them so much trash and sweet things, that they are sure to come back sick and cross for the rest of the day.' – And Mrs. Musgrove took the first opportunity of being alone with Anne, to say, 'Oh! Miss Anne, I cannot help wishing Mrs. Charles had a little of your method with those children. They are quite different creatures with you! But to be sure, in general they are so spoilt! It is a pity you cannot put your sister in the way of managing them. They are as fine healthy children as ever were seen, poor little dears, without partiality; but Mrs. Charles knows no more how they should be treated! – Bless me, how troublesome they are sometimes! – I assure you, Miss Anne, it prevents my wishing to see them at our house so often as I otherwise should. I believe Mrs. Charles is not quite pleased with my not inviting them oftener; but you know, it is very bad to have children with one, that one is obliged to be checking every moment: "don't do this, and don't do that;" – or that one can only keep in tolerable order by more cake than is good for them.'

She had this communication, moreover, from Mary. 'Mrs. Musgrove thinks all her servants so steady, that it would be high treason to call it in question; but I am sure, without exaggeration, that her upper house-maid and laundry-maid, instead of being in their business, are gadding about the village, all day long. I meet them wherever I go; and I declare, I never go twice into my nursery without seeing something of them. If Jemima were not the trustiest, steadiest creature in the world, it would be enough to spoil her; for she tells me, they are always tempting her to take a walk with them.' And on Mrs. Musgrove's side, it was, – 'I make a rule of never interfering in any of my daughter-in-law's concerns, for I know it would not do; but I shall tell *you*, Miss Anne, because you may be able to set things to rights, that I have no very good opinion of Mrs. Charles's nursery-maid: I hear strange stories of her; she is always upon the gad: and from my own knowledge, I can declare, she is such a fine-dressing lady, that she is enough to ruin any servants she comes near. Mrs. Charles quite swears by her, I know; but I just give you this hint, that you may be upon the watch; because, if you see any thing amiss, you need not be afraid of mentioning it.'

Again; it was Mary's complaint, that Mrs. Musgrove was very apt not to give her the precedence that was her due, when they dined at the Great House with other families; and she did not see any reason why she was to be considered so much at home as to lose her place. And one day, when Anne was walking with only the Miss Musgroves, one of them, after talking of rank, people of rank, and jealousy of rank, said, 'I have no scruple of observing to *you*, how nonsensical some persons are about their place, because all the world knows how easy and indifferent you are about it: but I wish any body could give Mary a hint that it would be a great deal better if she were not so very tenacious; especially, if she would not be always putting herself forward to take place of mamma. Nobody doubts her right to have precedence of mamma, but it would be more becoming in her not to be always insisting on it. It is not that mamma cares about it the least in the world, but I know it is taken notice of by many persons.'

How was Anne to set all these matters to rights? She could do little more than listen patiently, soften every grievance, and excuse each to the other, give them all hints of the forbearance necessary between such near neighbours, and make those hints broadest which were meant for her sister's benefit.

Not only is this slightly humorous, it serves to express something of that feeling for the relativity of truth in matters of conduct of which Jane Austen has such a lively awareness, and relativity of this kind serves to further complicate the problem of judgement. Nor is this an unnecessary complication; one must be alive to the point of view, the relativity of attitude, in formulating social judgements: one is considering relationships between individuals and individual expressions of these are necessarily relative to the point of view of the individuals concerned. It is another instance of Jane Austen's ability to realize the social and the individual as different faces of the same coin. But, although remarking this general effect of such passages, one notices the special sense of direction, the particular point of orientation from which valuable action is felt to proceed. How is Anne to act amidst this conflict of opinion? By giving 'them all hints of forbearance necessary between such near neighbours', yes, but especially to 'make those hints broadest which were meant for her sister's benefit'. Again family responsibility indicates where the emphasis is to fall.

The same remark might be made about the next striking passage of *self*-persuasion which occurs in the following chapter.

'So! You and I are to be left to shift by ourselves, with this poor sick child – and not a creature coming near us all the evening! I knew how it would be. This is always my luck! If there is any thing disagreeable going on, men are always sure to get out of it, and Charles is as bad as any of them. Very unfeeling! I must say it is very unfeeling of him, to be running away from his poor little boy; talks of his being going on so well! How does he know that he is going on well, or that there may not be a sudden change half an hour hence? I did not think Charles would have been so unfeeling. So, here he is to go away and enjoy himself, and because I am the poor mother, I am not to be allowed to stir; – and yet, I am sure, I am more unfit than any body else to be about the child. My being the mother is the very reason why my feelings should not be tried. I am not at all equal to it. You saw how hysterical I was yesterday.'

'But that was only the effect of the suddenness of your alarm – of the shock. You will not be hysterical again. I dare say we shall have nothing to distress us. I perfectly understand Mr. Robinson's directions, and have no fears; and indeed, Mary, I cannot wonder at your husband. Nursing does not belong to a man, it is not his province. A sick child is always the mother's property, her own feelings generally make it so.'

'I hope I am as fond of my child as any mother – but I do not know that I am of any more use in the sick-room than Charles, for I cannot be always scolding and teazing a poor child when it is ill; and you saw, this morning, that if I told him to keep quiet, he was sure to begin kicking about. I have not nerves for that sort of thing.'

'But, could you be comfortable yourself, to be spending the whole evening away from the poor boy?'

'Yes; you see his papa can, and why should not I? – Jemima is so careful! And she could send us word every hour how he was. I really think Charles might as well have told his father we would all come. I am not more alarmed about little Charles now than he is. I was dreadfully alarmed yesterday, but the case is very different to-day.'

'Well – if you do not think it too late to give notice for yourself, suppose you were to go, as well as your husband. Leave little Charles to my care. Mr. and Mrs. Musgrove cannot think it wrong, while I remain with him.'

'Are you serious?' cried Mary, her eyes brightening. 'Dear me! that's a very good thought, very good indeed. To be sure I may just as well go as not, for I am of no use at home – am I? and it only harasses me. You, who have not a mother's feelings, are a great deal the properest person. You can make little Charles do any thing; he always minds you at a word. It will be a great deal better than leaving him with only Jemima. Oh! I will certainly go; I am sure I ought if I can, quite as much as Charles, for they want me excessively to be acquainted with Captain Wentworth, and I know you do not mind being left alone. An excellent thought of yours, indeed, Anne! I will go and tell Charles, and get ready directly. You can send for us, you know, at a moment's notice, if any thing is the matter; but I dare say there will be nothing to alarm you. I should not go, you may be sure, if I did not feel quite at ease about my dear child.'

Here we have Mary busily justifying the satisfaction of her own desires at the expense of her maternal duties. The situation, broadly, recurs in Mary's letter to Anne in Chapter XVIII:

We have had a very dull Christmas; Mr. and Mrs. Musgrove have not had one dinner-party all the holidays. I do not reckon the Hayters as any body. The holidays, however, are over at last: I believe no children ever had such long ones. I am sure I had not. The house was cleared yesterday, except of the little Harvilles; but you will be surprised to hear they have never gone home. Mrs. Harville must be an odd mother to part with them so long. I do not understand it. They are not at all nice children, in my opinion; but Mrs. Musgrove seems to like them quite as well, if not better, than her grand-children. What dreadful weather we have had! It may not be felt in Bath, with your nice pavements; but in the country it is of some consequence. I have not had a creature call on me since the second week in January, except Charles Hayter, who has been calling much oftener than was welcome. Between ourselves, I think it a great pity Henrietta did not remain at Lyme as long as Louisa; it would have kept her a little out of his way. The carriage is gone to-day, to bring Louisa and the Harvilles to-morrow. We are not asked to dine with them, however, till the day after, Mrs. Musgrove is so afraid of her being fatigued by the journey, which is not very likely, considering the care that will be taken of her; and it would be much more convenient to me to dine there to-morrow. I am glad you find Mr. Elliot so agreeable, and wish I could be acquainted with him too; but I have my usual luck, I am always out of the way when any thing desirable is going on; always the last of my family to be noticed. What an immense time Mrs. Clay has been staying with Elizabeth! Does she never mean to go away? But perhaps if she were to leave the room vacant we might not be invited. Let me know what you think of this. I do not expect my children to be asked, you know. I can leave them at the Great House very well, for a month or six weeks.

Even whilst the prose of Jane Austen sweeps us from opinion to opposite opinion there is always present in the writing a recollection of the overriding standards against which these deviations, equivocations and persuasions, are to be judged and found wanting.

This raises the last of the complications which characterize the style of the novel – the sweep, but sometimes creep, from opinion to opposite opinion. This is most evident in the passages quoted above, but it is quite pervasive. Consider the two statements concerning Anne's attitudes towards the breaking off of her engagement to Wentworth in:

She was persuaded to believe the engagement a wrong thing: indiscreet, improper, hardly capable of success, and not deserving it.

She was persuaded that under every disadvantage of disapprobation at home, and every anxiety attending his profession, all their probable fears, delays, and disappointments, she should yet have been a happier woman in maintaining the engagement . . .

The same process, the same sway, affects the reader's mind, as in the case of Mary's self-justifications. Mary too appeals to the same criterion of her own happiness as is here directing Anne into a re-appraisal. It is not until later in the novel when this shifting opinion of Anne is more fully sketched in by the process at work in the characterization of Mary that the reader comes fully alive to the inadequacy of Anne's re-appraisal: what is wrong with it, of course, is the criterion appealed to, self-happiness. And just as Mary's re-appraisals of her duties offend against that criterion of family obligation (maternal duty), so Anne's re-appraisal here offends against the duty she properly owes to the respectable Lady Russell, her 'adopted' parent. The justness of Anne's earlier decision is then pressed home when Louisa meets with her accident at Lyme and we have Wentworth uttering the unconsciously ironic cries:

'Had I done as I ought! But so eager and resolute! Dear, sweet Louisa!'

Lest we miss the irony the narrator underlines it for us:

> Anne wondered whether it ever occurred to him now, to question the justness of his own previous opinion as to the universal felicity and advantage of firmness of character; and whether it might not strike him that, like all other qualities of the mind, it should have its proportions and limits. She thought it could scarcely escape him to feel that a persuadable temper might sometimes be as much in favour of happiness as a very resolute character.

'Happiness' here is being used in a different sense from that in which earlier Anne could seem to chide herself for not giving way to the pursuit of her own happiness, the way in which Mary does.

The central concern of the novel, indicated in its title, is the appreciation and assessment of those intricate dispositions of the mind that sway us to action and the relationship between these dispositions (which are individual) and the social fabric. How do they mesh into the fabric in order to enhance or diminish its value? And all the complexities so insistently stressed in this too brief account, and which are part of the make-up of Jane Austen's vision, need to be closely traced, examined and judged if we are to be persuaded that *Persuasion* does arrive at a satisfactory answer to this kind of question.

The Romanticism of Coleridge

A reading of Wordsworth and Jane Austen might well suggest that in the early years of the nineteenth century literature in England had discovered its proper business and had established 'a central, a truly human point of view' for the literature of the nineteenth century. But there were other equally important and what were to prove more influential tendencies in the literature of the late eighteenth and early-nineteenth centuries, tendencies which serve to place Wordsworth and Jane Austen as the culminating moments of the eighteenth century, of a world not yet convulsed by the painful and horrific experience of the industrial revolution and unaffected by the questioning of artistic worth and artistic vision to which the new iron age gave rise.

These tendencies are those associated with a dominant mood of Romanticism, with a strange complex of feelings and attitudes, a passion compounded of self-despair and self-elevation, of gross insensitivity and a tormented and tormenting vision, of horror and bathos, all isolating and racking the individual as artist or as an aspirant to art. The mood is set by Wordsworth's poetical partner, Coleridge, and will eventually blacken into the 'modern' mood of so much twentieth-century literature.

Samuel Taylor Coleridge was a man of many talents, all of the second order; he was a poet, a philosopher, a critic and a theologian of sorts. His desire to be a poet, and not just a poet but an important poet, seems to have been considerable and dominant. Unfortunately, his real but limited talent for poetry came to maturity late and was more or less exhausted by the time he was thirty. This is by no means an uncommon occurrence: many young men with aspirations to poetry find that the vein runs out within a few years. I doubt, however, that many would seek to turn this experience of ebbing talent into poetry, as Coleridge does in *Dejection Ode*, which makes that poem if not unique at least very peculiar. The poem is peculiar, anyway: you can't bring much imagination to a lament for the loss of your powers of imagination. If you can, then you find yourself in a paradoxical situation and one which provides support for Plato's contention that poets are liars.

The *Ode* was composed when Coleridge was thirty; it looks back upon an earlier period of the poet's life, when he was still capable of transmuting afflictions by the power of Fancy, from a time when Fancy has fled and the 'shaping spirit of Imagination' has been suspended. All of which is summed-up in a stanza:

> There was a time when, though my path was rough,
>   This joy within me dallied with distress,
> And all misfortunes were but as the stuff
>   Whence Fancy made me dreams of happiness:
> For hope grew round me, like the twining vine,
> And fruits, and foliage, not my own, seemed mine.
> But now afflictions bow me down to earth:
> Nor care I that they rob me of my mirth;
>   But oh! each visitation
> Suspends what nature gave me at my birth,
>   My shaping spirit of Imagination.

This is a stanza which I have chosen as an introduction to Coleridge's poetry. It draws attention to the importance of the Fancy in the period of the poet's fruitfulness and to Coleridge's eventual recognition that he was lacking in the 'shaping spirit of Imagination'. It also introduces the distinction between Fancy and Imagination which Wordsworth and Coleridge considered of such crucial importance in determining the nature and value of poetry.

In the *Ode*, Coleridge is being guided by a theory about poetic insight which he shared with and may have derived from Wordsworth, his poetical partner. In 1802, the year in which Coleridge composed the *Dejection Ode*, lamenting the suspension of the 'shaping spirit of Imagination' which nature had given him at birth, Wordsworth wrote the following in his Ode: *Intimations of Immortality from Recollections of Early Childhood*:

> Our birth is but a sleep and a forgetting:
> The Soul that rises with us, our life's Star,
>   Hath had elsewhere its setting,
>   And cometh from afar:
>   Not in entire forgetfulness,
>   And not in utter nakedness,
> But trailing clouds of glory do we come
>   From God, who is our home:

> Heaven lies about us in our infancy!
> Shades of the prison-house begin to close
>   Upon the growing Boy
> But he beholds the light, and whence if flows,
>   He sees it in his joy;
> The Youth, who daily farther from the east
>   Must travel, still is Nature's Priest,
>   And by the vision splendid
>   Is on his way attended:
> At length the Man perceives it die away,
> And fade into the light of common day.

The doctrine propounded in these lines is essentially Platonic, although bowdlerised by Christianity into what is commonly referred to as Christian Platonism. It represents the soul as immortal and as coming down from Heaven to inhabit the prison of the flesh at birth. Initially it is inspired by recollections of its proper home, Heaven, but in the common course of ordinary life it becomes tarnished and corrupted until eventually it loses its original awareness and vision. It is to this awareness and vision that Wordsworth and Coleridge give the name Imagination. So that the Imagination, then, is a power of insight and understanding with which we are born; it is, in Coleridge's phrase, 'What nature gave me at my birth'. It is not only a 'shaping spirit', the fount of all truly creative activity, its essential characteristic is visionary, it enables us (in a phrase Wordsworth uses elsewhere) 'to see into the heart of things', to see things as they really are and not simply as they appear to be. In this it is quite distinct from mere Fancy, which allows us to manufacture an order of things but not to perceive 'things as they really are'.

All of which is by way of explanation and not by way of justification. The doctrine is philosophically specious, but that is neither here nor there, for as T. S. Eliot once observed,

> A philosophical theory which has entered into poetry is established, for its truth or falsity in one sense ceases to matter, and its truth in another sense is proved.

We are concerned with the doctrine of Imagination and Fancy only as organizational fictions, although in the case of Wordsworth and Coleridge they bear directly upon the poet's own appreciation of his poetry.

So it is in the *Dejection Ode* with Coleridge; he sees himself not as a poet gifted with a persistent visionary power, but as a man like other men, and looking to his Imagination,

> At length the Man perceives it die away
> And fade into the light of common day.

That at least is Coleridge's estimation of his own poetic fate in the *Dejection Ode*. Poets, however, are notoriously bad at appraising their own work. We can appreciate the feeling of Coleridge at the thought of losing his poetic powers, and to make sure we do the poem spells it out for us; it is

> A grief without a pang, void, dark, and drear,
> A stifled, drowsy, unimpassioned grief,
> Which finds no natural outlet, no relief,
> In word, or sigh, or tear . . .

Nevertheless, in diagnosing the cause of the decline in his creative power and suggesting that it is to be found in the growth of his intellectual interests, the poem for a moment catches the tone of what Wordsworth called 'the still sad music of humanity'.

> For not to think of what I needs must feel,
> But to be still and patient, all I can;
> And haply by abstruse research to steal
> From my own nature all the natural man –
> This was my sole resource, my only plan:
> Till that which suits a part infects the whole,
> And now is almost grown the habit of my soul.

The lines make a fine and fitting epitaph to Coleridge's career as a poet. They mark a deliberate movement away from poetic activity, with its continuous conjunction of thought and feeling, a deliberate and planned decision 'not to think of what I needs must feel', and an equally deliberate resolve to pursue an intellectual career, in which thought is abstracted from feeling, a deliberate decision 'by abstruse research to steal / From my own nature all the natural man'. The consequence of these decisions has been to establish a habit of mind ('the habit of my soul', as Coleridge calls it) which, in abstracting thought from feeling, has suspended the 'shaping spirit of the Imagination'.

It certainly seems to be a general truth that the cultivation of intellectual interests is fatal to poetic talent; Pope was uttering a commonplace when he remarked that poetical wit and intellectual judgement are often at strife. Why it should be so, I'm not sure, and it seems pointless to speculate. It is enough that Coleridge is an instance of this and that the *Dejection Ode* marks the point at which his career takes a new course, bent now towards criticism and philosophy, and philosophy, as Keats observed, 'will clip an angel's wings, empty the haunted air and gnomed mind'.

The *Ode*, however, also provides us with an appreciation by the poet of his fruitful period, the two years 1797 and 1798, which saw the composition of the *Ancient Mariner, Christabel, Kubla Khan, Frost at Midnight*, and the publication, with Wordsworth, of *Lyrical Ballads*. This was the period, presumably, when (in the words of the *Ode*),

> all misfortunes were but as the stuff
> Whence Fancy made me dreams of happiness,

when

> hope grew round me, like the twining vine,
> And fruits, and foliage, not my own, seemed mine.

It seems that Coleridge is placing the products of his most fruitful poetic period as works of Fancy, as belonging (that is to say) to the lower and not the higher order of poetry. Again, the poet may be wrong in this appreciation of his work, but since the distinction between the two orders of poetry was one to which Wordsworth and Coleridge had given a great deal of consideration, it is an appreciation to be taken as a serious and thoughtful one.

I have already mentioned the distinction drawn between fancy and imagination; in general terms, it is better and more succinctly expressed by Ruskin than by Wordsworth or Coleridge. 'The fancy,' Ruskin explained, 'sees the outside. . . . The imagination sees the heart and inner nature, and makes them felt.' To fill out that definition, it needs to be added that fancy is associated with the power of invention, the ability to 'dream things up' or to place existing things in new patterns of relationship; the imagination is associated, on the other hand, with perception and insight. Fancy, then, is concerned with *giving* significance to things; imagination is concerned with revealing the actual significance of things.

This distinction occupied the attention of Wordsworth and Coleridge in planning and reshaping their joint publication, *Lyrical Ballads*, which first appeared anonymously in 1798. Their discussions appear to have been wide-ranging and convoluted and it would not be to the point here to attempt to summarize them. It is, I think, fair and sufficient to say that in the course of these discussions Coleridge's contributions to the collection were reduced and their position in the volume changed and that the effect of these alterations was to place Coleridge's poems in the shadow of Wordsworth's. In the process, the distinction between the nature of their contributions was firmly drawn: Wordsworth was to provide poems of the Imagination and Coleridge was to provide poems of the Fancy. In other words, Coleridge's appreciation of imaginative poetry and his recognition that his own was poetry of the fancy was formed in this period of discussion between 1798 and 1800 (when the second and revised edition of *Lyrical Ballads* appeared) and this appreciation and recognition was sharpened if not produced by placing his own work alongside that of Wordsworth.

Although *Lyrical Ballads* first appeared anonymously (and was, incidentally, well enough received by the reviewers), the distinction between the works of the two contributors was noted. It was felt that readers, coming to *The Ancient Mariner*, ploughed through the poem and then gave up, not continuing to read further and therefore not reading those poems of Wordsworth which appeared after *The Ancient Mariner* in the first edition. Wordsworth and Coleridge, therefore, decided to move *The Ancient Mariner* to the end.

Later this distinction between the two very different kinds of poetry present in *Lyrical Ballads* tended to be played down and the collection spoken of as though it were cut from a common cloth. The volume assumed an historical significance in literature which tended to obscure its poetical character. It is not difficult to appreciate why this should be so, but although the publication of *Lyrical Ballads* may be said to have inaugurated the Romantic Movement in England, it is almost impossible to draw a line such that *Tintern Abbey* belongs more obviously with *The Ancient Mariner* than it does with Alexander Pope's *Windsor Forest*. With the Romantic Revival far enough in the past now to allow of some critical perspective, it is becoming more widely recognized that

Wordsworth's poetry has as much and probably more in common with, say, Pope's than it has with that of Coleridge.

What Wordsworth and Coleridge do have in common, at least in *Lyrical Ballads*, is a sense of poetical mission; both of them, incidentally, looked upon poets as seers and prophets, a view which became characteristic of the Romantics. It is a view which proves a great handicap to a poet, as may be noticed from a reading of Spenser and Milton, who also looked upon themselves as poetical missionaries. The Romantics, not surprisingly, looked back to Spenser and Milton as predecessors of the Romantic Movement. What they have in common is that they take themselves so very seriously that their poetry is entirely humourless. Unfortunately for them, though not I think for us, such a persistent and consistent seriousness is quite contrary to the genius of the English language. The result is that this imp of English from time to time takes its revenge and reduces moments of intended high seriousness to comedy.

This, then, is something that Wordsworth and Coleridge do have in common; they are both victims of the genius of the language. In the poetry of both, comedy asserts itself as bathos; fortunately undetected and hence unexpunged by both poets, who were victimized in this special way by their own solemnity. That it was a solemnity about their own poetry rather than a general and inherent deficiency is evident in Coleridge's case. Coleridge dismissed such verses as

> I put my hat upon my head
> And went into the Strand
> And there I met another man
> Whose hat was in his hand.

because, as he remarked, 'they are empty of all sense and feeling'. What he failed to appreciate was the similarity between that piece of nonsense verse and this:

> The Sun came up upon the left,
> Out of the sea came he!
> And he shone bright, and on the right
> Went down into the sea,

which is a stanza of *The Ancient Mariner*.

As a critic, too, Coleridge was alive to his partner's lapses and remarked that Wordsworth's seriousness is at times greater than the subject will allow. In a perceptive criticism of 'I wandered lonely as a cloud', he observed that in the passage

> They flash upon the inward eye,
> Which is the bliss of solitude;
> And then my heart with pleasure fills,
> And dances with the daffodils,

the balance of seriousness tips and the final two lines become bathetic. He fails to notice, however, that the same is true of

> The moving Moon went up the sky,
> And nowhere did abide:
> Softly she was going up,
> And a star or two beside.

The stanza, again, is from *The Ancient Mariner*.

There are several notorious instances of bathos in Wordsworth's poetry, of course. In *Simon Lee* there is the infamous example,

> For still, the more he works, the more
> His poor old ankles swell,

and in *The Thorn*, the equally infamous lines on a puddle:

> I've measured it from side to side:
> 'Tis three feet long, and two feet wide.

But bathos is endemic in the poetry of the Romantic Revival and one of my own favourite instances is not from Wordsworth or Coleridge but from Shelley's *Ode to the West Wind*. The *Ode* finds Shelley in the same Aeolian mood as Coleridge in *Dejection*; in the fifth and final section it climbs towards its climax and then, in the very final line, slips on a banana skin cast by the genius of the language and crashes down into bathos:

> Drive my dead thoughts over the universe,
> Like withered leaves, to quicken a new birth;
> And, by the incantation of this verse,

Scatter, as from an unextinguished hearth
Ashes and sparks, my words among mankind!
Be through my lips to unawakened earth

The trumpet of a prophecy! O wind,
If Winter comes, can Spring be far behind?

I am aware, of course, that the whole poem operates upon a suppressed metaphor and that the final line is intended to be taken metaphorically. It is typical of the Romantics, however, that Shelley should be so intent upon a portentous metaphor that he fails to appreciate the devastating effect of the literal sense of the language. That imp I have mentioned, that genius of the language, ensures that at the crucial moment, when the poet is making his grand gesture in the finale, the commonplace, literal sense of the language asserts itself and cannot be suppressed, nor with it the smile of those who take the final revelation in its impish, English sense:

O wind,
If Winter comes, can Spring be far behind?

Let me give one final example from yet another Romantic poet, Keats; not because it takes us any further forward in our consideration of Coleridge, I suspect, but simply because it is delightful in itself. The bathos here is the result of distorting normal English syntax in order to achieve a rhyme; it is from another ode, the *Ode on a Grecian Urn*. You may recall that the poem refers to fair maidens and bold lovers:

Bold Lover, never, never canst thou kiss,
Though winning near the goal – yet, do not grieve;
She cannot fade, though thou hast not thy bliss,
For ever wilt thou love, and she be fair!

So there we have the lovers doomed to an eternity of frustration, which I would have thought was only rendered the more acute by the fact that the maiden remains for ever fair and so, presumably, forever desirable. The next reference to these unfortunates occurs in the final stanza:

O Attic shape! Fair attitude! with brede
Of marble men and maidens overwrought.

Again one cannot suppress the image which the mischievous imp of the language so readily supplies: if the men are marble, no wonder the maidens are overwrought!

Bathos, then, is a regular feature of the poetry of the Romantic Revival and in his occasional strictures upon Wordsworth's poetry Coleridge shows himself to have been aware of this. Nevertheless, he seems to have been unconscious of his own bathetic lapses:

> The silly buckets on the deck,
> That had so long remained,
> I dreamt that they were filled with dew;
> And when I awoke, it rained.

There is, however, an important distinction (I believe) between Wordsworth's lapses and those of Coleridge. Wordsworth's appear to be the result of too much imagination, of over-absorption in his subject; Coleridge's, on the other hand, seem to be due to an absorbing concern for surface finish, usually for getting the rhyme or the metre correct. Coleridge's contributions to *Lyrical Ballads* have a character which sets them aside immediately from those of Wordsworth. His best and best known contribution, *The Rime of the Ancient Mariner*, has all the 'artfulness' of a painting; we are held, like the wedding guest, by the glittering eye, and our attention is riveted upon 'a painted ship upon a painted ocean' or upon the colourful picture of the water snakes,

> Blue, glossy green, and velvet black
> They coil'd and swam, and every track
>   Was a flash of golden fire.

A similar effect is produced by *Lewti*, intended as one of Coleridge's contributions to *Lyrical Ballads* but dropped in favour of *The Nightingale*; its attempt to invest inanimate nature with human purpose and significance results only in a string of pictorial analogies.

The distinction between the poetry of Coleridge and Wordsworth in *Lyrical Ballads* is that that of Coleridge is intent upon the picturesque whilst that of Wordsworth is engaged in revealing human significance within seemingly nonhuman material. The latter process is described in Wordsworth's *Lines left upon a seat in a Yew-tree*:

> on these barren rocks, with juniper,
> And heath, and thistle, thinly sprinkl'd o'er,
> Fixing his downward eye, he many an hour
> A morbid pleasure nourished, tracing here
> An emblem of his own unfruitful life.

The description is not exact; Wordsworth's poems are not in any pictorial sense emblematic: the nature which his contemplation of natural objects reveals is human nature and not an emblem of it. So it is that our greatest Nature poet can quite truthfully claim that the mind of man is the haunt and main region of his poetry.

Coleridge's poetry lacks this kind of inner seriousness; what seriousness the poetic subjects have is *brought to* not *unfolded from* them by the poet. It is because Coleridge appears to be importing significance into his poetry that his attempts to point a moral fall flat and strike us as irrelevant, even slightly ridiculous. The most obvious, indeed glaring instance of this is (of course) to be found in one of the concluding stanzas of *The Ancient Mariner*. Having finished his story, the Mariner bids the wedding guest farewell with a piece of advice culled from the experience he has related in his tale:

> He prayeth best who loveth best,
> All things both great and small:
> For the dear God, who loveth us,
> He made and loveth all.

Now, however one defines the limitations of *The Rime of the Ancient Mariner*, and I have given some idea of how I would do so, its achievement can by no means be reduced to the level to which Coleridge himself reduces it in this moral tag. There are no objections, I am sure, to the sentiment expressed in the Mariner's last words and I am as willing as the next man to cherish 'all things both great and small'. But in the context of what has gone before, a sudden deflation occurs here as the poem poses as a message from the R.S.P.C.A.

I should, perhaps, pause here to say something about *The Rime of the Ancient Mariner*, if only to correct widespread misunderstandings which are due to a simple failure to grasp the general character of the poem. The poem is intended to be read as an early sixteenth-century ballad: the marginal gloss makes this quite evident, not only by the fact that it is there but also in its fairly successful imitation of early-Tudor English.

There are, in any case, sufficient linguistic clues throughout the poem: *quoth he, eftsoons, uprist, I wist, gramercy, a-feared*, etc. In addition to which we have what might be called the 'furniture' of the poem, the bassoon and the merry minstrelsy of the wedding feast, the reference to the witch's oils and to the dungeon's grate (i.e. grating), and above all to the Mariner's firearm, the cross-bow. The historical placing is also implicit in the religious context provided by references to vespers, penance, shrieving, Heaven's Mother, Mary Queen, the holy rood, the Hermit who 'crossed his brow', and to 'my kind saint'. Perhaps the most conclusive evidence, certainly the most obvious, is provided in the marginal gloss, 'the ship enters the Pacific Ocean', which stands beside the lines,

> We were the first that ever burst
> Into that silent sea.

Recognition of the fact that the poem is an imitation of a sixteenth century ballad forestalls a great deal of critical confusion. The awareness which the poem seeks to recreate is that of an early-Tudor mariner, an awareness compounded of traditional, medieval Catholicism and superstition. In this respect, the poem seems to me to be extremely successful.

Once the character of the poem has been appreciated a great deal of its mystery disappears, or rather assumes a different significance from that afforded it by those intent upon treating it as an elaborate piece of symbolism. If the poem still strikes us as mysterious, this is a comment upon the mariner's state of consciousness. It needs to be realized that a large part of Coleridge's success in the poem is due to his ability to recreate this state of consciousness and convince us that it is historically credible. The sense of the mysterious we are presented with in the poem is (I believe) very close to that of an early-Tudor mariner. What is not credible is the tepid moral conclusion drawn by such a person from his experience at sea. That, however, is a more contentious and less important judgement than that concerning the adequacy of the moral tag as a summary of the reader's response to the poem. Indeed,

> He prayeth best who loveth best,
> All things both great and small:
> For the dear God, who loveth us,
> He made and loveth all,

may be placed alongside such an earlier stanza as,

> The naked hulk alongside came,
> And the twain were casting dice,
> 'The game is done! I've won! I've won!'
> Quoth she, and whistles thrice.

Both may be said to be yet further instances of the poem's descent into bathos, and the list of such instances is now becoming considerable enough, I feel, to provide its own judgement upon the poem.

It is not my intention to rub Coleridge's nose in the moral of his poem; it is probably better to note the comparison with Wordsworth and leave the matter there, within the covers of *Lyrical Ballads*. With Wordsworth the 'moral' grows out of the treatment and attention given to the subject. Thus, in lines from the conclusion of the poem I've already mentioned, *Lines left upon a seat in a Yew-tree* (not, incidentally, one of Wordsworth's better poems) Wordsworth underscores the failing of the unfruitful recluse without the slightest distraction of our attention, for our attention has been fixed throughout upon the significance of the tree and its environs:

> Stranger! henceforth be warned; and know, that pride,
> Howe'er disguised in its own majesty,
> Is littleness; that he, who feels contempt
> For any living thing, hath faculties
> Which he has never used; that thought to him
> Is in its infancy. The man, whose eye
> Is ever on himself, doth look on one,
> The least of nature's works . . .

The 'moral', you will notice, is very similar to that which Coleridge tacks onto *The Ancient Mariner*, but Wordsworth can (like Pope) stoop to moralize his song without lowering its importance. And it is not by accident, I believe, that the morality of Wordsworth is more profound than that of his friend; it is the result of a profounder insight, which reveals itself in the slow and sad assurance of Wordsworth's characteristic blank verse.

No other poet as was remarked earlier can make plain and simple English so continuously majestic and no other poet (Shakespeare included) can use blank verse as naturally and as finely as Wordsworth.

So it is unfortunate that history should force Coleridge to face such a comparison.

If we turn back to *Dejection Ode* we can diminish the effect of that comparison. There seems little doubt that Coleridge had hopes or dreams of becoming an important poet: if that was not so the dejection of the *Ode* would hardly have the force and the paradoxical direction that it does have. At the same time, the *Ode* records Coleridge's own recognition that his poetical achievements had been limited to works of Fancy. Looking back, then, he sees the poems of 1797 and 1798 for what they are: poems of the lower order. He never challenged comparison with his friend and was fully conscious that Wordsworth was a major poet and he himself was but a minor one. Quite evidently this was a bitter truth to him, but it is one he came to recognize clearly in the years between 1798 and 1802. In 1802, in the *Dejection Ode*, he also recognizes that his own poetical hopes had been grounded upon nothing more substantial than these works of Fancy; it was, the *Ode* records,

> Fancy made me dreams of happiness.

In short, by 1802, Coleridge was aware that the poems of his fruitful period were works of Fancy and that these had aroused in him hopes which, because they were false, had faded. An essential ingredient in Coleridge's dejection, therefore, is the sad truth that (as Keats wrote in *Ode to a Nightingale*)

> the fancy cannot cheat so well
> As she is famed to do, deceiving elf.

Coleridge's own awareness in *Dejection Ode* guards him, therefore, against the consequences of a straight comparison between his poetry and that of Wordsworth. Coleridge has pre-empted the force of that comparison. In doing so he has also demonstrated the new direction of his interest and talent. To be able to place the achievement of his poetry and his poetical aspirations as 'fanciful' instances the kind of critical intelligence which henceforths directs his career.

It is strange that of the two contributors to *Lyrical Ballads*, it should be the disciple rather than the master whose poetry placed its peculiar stamp upon English Romanticism. It is Coleridge, in poems such as *Love* and *Christabel*, who sponsors that interest in the medieval, which so influences Keats and Tennyson. And, in *Kubla Khan*, it is Coleridge who fosters that interest in the exotic which we meet again in Shelley and in Keats. But to Coleridge more than to any other single poet, the Romantics owe that characteristic mixture of the wild, the exotic and the gothic. *Kubla Khan* is a combination of these seemingly disparate elements. It begins in the exotic setting of Xanadu:

> In Xanadu did Kubla Khan
> A stately pleasure-dome decree:
> Where Alph, the sacred river, ran
> Through caverns measureless to man
>   Down to a sunless sea.

It proceeds to a description which actually defines wild and savage natural scenery as *romantic*:

> But oh! that deep romantic chasm which slanted
> Down the green hill athwart a cedarn cover!
> A savage place!

And then, taking the hint from that last phrase, it moves into the world of the gothic novel:

> A savage place! as holy and enchanted
> As e'er beneath a waning moon was haunted
> By woman wailing for her demon-lover!

The remainder of the poem moves back and forth between these three basic elements, the wild, the exotic and the gothic, in a way which defines the special and distinctive range of Romantic poetry.

According to Coleridge the poem, *Kubla Khan*, came to him in a dream. He had been reading an old travel book, *Purchas his Pilgrimage*, when he fell asleep in his chair and dreamt the poem. On awaking he remembered it all, some two to three hundred lines, and began to write it down. As he was doing so he was interrupted by a visitor 'on business from Porlock' and when he returned to the task had forgotten the remainder of the poem. Coleridge's account, however, has been called into question and, except as an instance of the Romantics' belief in the spontaneity with which poetry was created, is of little importance to an understanding of *Kubla Khan*. It does draw our attention to the poem's unfinished state and, I suppose, may be taken as an excuse for this.

However, from our point of view, the poem is of interest as a prototype of Romantic poetry, written at a time (1798) when Coleridge's powers were on the eve of the decline recorded in the *Dejection Ode*. We could, in fact, interpret Coleridge's own account of its creation as evidence of a decline of his Fancy, for it seems the poem remained unfinished because Coleridge lacked the power of invention to complete it. This appears to be admitted in the poem itself:

> A damsel with a dulcimer
> In a vision once I saw:
> It was an Abyssinian maid,
> And on her dulcimer she played,
> Singing of mount Abora.
> Could I revive within me
> Her symphony and song,
> To such a deep delight 'twould win me,
> That with music loud and long,
> I would build that dome in air . . .

Could I revive within me looks forward to that suspension of the shaping spirit lamented in the *Dejection Ode*.

Yet even as the poem remarks its own failure to achieve poetic revival, it is providing the larger Romantic Revival with its own distinctive complexion and with its own peculiar image of itself. It is not the image Wordsworth provides: detached, contemplative, brooding and sombre. When we think of the Romantic poet and picture him in our mind's eye, the usual image that forms is that of the poet as drawn by Coleridge: a man possessed with a divine frenzy that seems to smoulder within him, making its presence felt in 'the glittering eye'. In fact, that phrase, from the description of the ancient mariner, brings to our attention how well the mariner fits the romantic image of the poet as a man possessed with a vision that he must unburden himself of – as Coleridge struggles to do in *Kubla Khan* and Shelley in *Ode to the West Wind*. It is the image of the poet as the 'mad lutanist' of the *Dejection Ode*; the image which the poet would like to entertain of himself, according to the conclusion of *Kubla Khan*:

> And all should cry, Beware! Beware!
> His flashing eyes, his floating hair!

> Weave a circle round him thrice,
> And close your eyes with holy dread,
> For he on honey-dew hath fed,
> And drunk the milk of Paradise.

Not until Coleridge does the poet become such a wild, daemonic creature: an outward manifestation of romantic inspiration, romantic passion or, what has been called, romantic *angst*.

There is little in the poetry of Wordsworth that conforms to European Romanticism, with its love of the grotesque, the macabre, the violent and its undercurrent of horror. The strain of European Romanticism seems to enter English poetry through Coleridge. The contorted, striving and almost tortured shapes of European Romantic painting have their counterpart in English Romantic poetry in lines such as Coleridge's:

> And from this chasm, with ceaseless turmoil seething,
> As if this earth in fast thick pants were breathing,
> A mighty fountain momently was forced:
> Amid whose swift half-intermitted burst
> Huge fragments vaulted like rebounding hail . . .

Just as in Romantic painting, so in lines such as these, the classical stillness and careful poise of the eighteenth century is exploded; and those who wish to look upon poetry as 'an image of the times' will find the image here. The eruption which takes place in these lines, shattering the orderliness of eighteenth-century art, is more truly a reflection of that other, political eruption than is the occasionally expressed enthusiasm for the French Revolution, such as Wordsworth's,

> France standing on the top of golden hours
> And human nature seeming born again.

The political opinions of the poets were susceptible to change; the change in sensibility instanced in those lines from *Kubla Khan* was irrevocable.

The writhing figures of European Romanticism are accompanied by the macabre and horrific, the vision of which is central to Coleridge's *Ancient Mariner*, as it is to Keats's *Pot of Basil*, where Isabella takes the severed head of her lover,

> Then in a silken scarf, – sweet with the dews
>   Of precious flowers pluck'd in Araby,
> And divine liquids with odorous ooze
>   Through the cold serpent-pipe refreshfully, –
> She wrapped it up; and for its tomb did choose
>   A garden-pot, wherein she laid it by,
> And cover'd it with mould, and o'er it set
> Sweet Basil, which her tears kept ever wet.

The macabre becomes horrific when Thomas Hood's Ulysses breaks a branch on Circe's island and blood pumps out of the tree, and when the soul is struck with guilt in Tennyson's *Palace of Art* and discovers that

> In dark corners of her palace stood
>   Uncertain shapes; and unawares
> On white-eyed phantasms weeping tears of blood,
>   And horrible nightmares
>
> And hollow shades enclosing hearts of flame,
>   And, with dim fretted foreheads all,
> On corpses three-months old at noon she came
>   That stood against the wall.

By the time Coleridgean romanticism has reached the early Tennyson, *via* Keats, even the poor house-mouse shrieks in the wainscot.

   All of which leads one to reappraise if not the value at least the importance of Coleridge's poetry. It was Coleridge and not Wordsworth, the minor and not the major poet, who made the English Romantic Revival a part of European Romanticism, who brought to it the romantic *angst*, what Mario Praz has called 'the romantic agony'. It is an agony which informs the *Dejection Ode* as the poet turns from his thoughts, 'Reality's dark dream', to reality itself, 'a scream of agony by torture lengthened out'. Faced by which he asks the wind,

> Thou mighty Poet, e'en to frenzy bold!
>   What tell's thou now about?

and receives the answer, of

> groans of trampled men, with smarting wounds –
> At once they groan with pain, and shudder with the cold!

It is the same romantic, agonizing vision as we have already noticed in Tennyson's *Palace of Art*, and it is the same as that we meet with in Keats's *Ode to a Nightingale*, a vision of

> The weariness, the fever, and the fret
>   Here, where men sit and hear each other groan;
> Where palsy shakes a few, sad, last grey hairs,
>   Where youth grows pale, and spectre-thin, and dies;
>   Where but to think is to be full of sorrow
>   And leaden-eyed despairs,
> Where Beauty cannot keep her lustrous eyes,
>   Or new Love pine at them beyond tomorrow.

I end as I began, then, with the *Dejection Ode*, with the agony it bequeaths to Keats and Tennyson and with which Coleridge places English Romanticism within European Romanticism. To do so, I believe, is to make the point that whereas the intrinsic merit of Coleridge's poetry is much as it is judged to be in the *Ode*, nevertheless it has an extrinsic importance far in excess of its own slender merits. What I have tried to show is that this is so and that if we approach the Romantic experience in England through a reading of Coleridge's poetry, we give to this Romanticism a sense it would not have if we approached it through a reading of Wordsworth. Wordsworth is unquestioningly the greater poet and yet, although his influence was great and often (as in John Stuart Mill's case) liberating, it was susceptible to trivialization, to easy pollution by the notion that it established poetry as being properly centred upon birds and bees and flowers. As one schoolboy said to another, on being told to take out their poetry books, 'Here we go! More hey-nonny-no and bloody daffodils!' That exclamation reveals a prevalent, romantic conception of poetry which is exploded once we begin to look upon Romanticism in a Coleridgean light.

Mill and *Laissez-faire*

Whilst Coleridge's romanticism did much to shape individual sensibilities in the nineteenth century, his social thinking served also to moderate the kind of hard-headed eighteenth-century individualism epitomized by Bentham. John Stuart Mill's essays on Bentham and Coleridge indicate how this moderation worked and their relevance to a proper appreciation of nineteenth-century literature has been forcibly argued by F. R. Leavis in his introduction to *Mill on Bentham and Coleridge*. Although in important respects Leavis's argument is unsound, in general his view of the study of literature as a base camp rather than a concentration camp for criticism would meet with wide, if not universal, agreement. A proper appreciation of literature, after all, does require an awareness of complexities of attitude and feeling and that is a requirement which must be met by any worthwhile occupation in other spheres of intellectual life. It is for this reason that the critical intelligence can lay claim to being the central, organizing intelligence of an age.

It is this point of view which informs Leavis's introductory essay; a point of view which he applies to the study of the nineteenth century and illustrates with reference not only to Bentham, Coleridge and Mill, but to men such as Cobbett, Carlyle and Arnold, and women such as 'George Eliot' and Beatrice Webb. Indeed, one of the prime purposes of Leavis's essay is to draw the central figures of the period into significant relationship. Apart from advancing an argument of a general kind, therefore, Leavis's essay also offers something like a study-guide to the central flow of civilization in nineteenth-century England.

The character of the essay as a guide to further study is marred in the first instance by a too loose and easy appeal to influences. There is something all too familiar about the manner in which, in the following passage, 'we establish a line running from Coleridge and the German historical critics through Thomas to Matthew Arnold' and then to George Eliot.

Of another early contact, of Mill's [writes Leavis] the effects were overt and indisputable, that which began in

"1828 and 1829, when the Coleridgians, in the persons of Maurice and Sterling, made their appearance in the Society as a second Liberal and even Radical party, on totally different grounds from Benthamism and vehemently opposed to it; bringing into these discussions the general doctrines and modes of thought of the European reaction against the philosophy of the eighteenth century."

This refers back, of course, to the two essays. But it also adds very notably to the system of significant relations. For with Maurice, Christian Socialism and Arnold of Rugby appear on the map, and though (aided by the irresponsible Stracheyan *procede*) we tend to let the ethos of *Tom Brown's Schooldays* stand for Thomas Arnold, his son has much closer affinities with him than is commonly supposed. So we establish a line running from Coleridge and the German historical critics through Thomas to Matthew Arnold, thus connecting the last – as there is point in doing – with his father's Broad Church liberalism.

The line is extended to George Eliot in a footnote:

A line very relevant to George Eliot's development: in fact, for the understanding of her intellectual and religious background, L. Trilling's *Matthew Arnold* provides a valuable supplement to Leslie Stephen's *George Eliot*.

The suspicion this manner of proceeding gives rise to is that which leads the critic to cock a sceptical eye at the efforts of all too many literary historians. The nominations are both too glib and too provincial. Are we to understand that the influence which flows through the Rev. F. D. Maurice, and presumably Canon Kingsley, is to be equated with or given the same weight as that of the German historical critics, of (say) Hegel and Feuerbach? The idea is ludicrous.

Leavis's – and for that matter Mill's – conception of what constitutes a significant relationship in the intellectual life of a period has been broadly accepted. Marxism, however, rejects the view, implicit in Mill and explicit in Leavis, that the truly significant relationships of an age are relationships between minds or 'modes of thought'. It does not 'to the marriage of true minds admit impediment', but it does expose the error of looking upon significant history – the history that in the last resort really counts – as the history of ideas and opinions.

An illustration of this manner of doing business with history may be found in the following quotation from Mill's essay on Bentham; it is representative of a general attitude in which Mill and Leavis share:

> . . . to Bentham more than to any other source might be traced the questioning spirit, the disposition to demand the *why* of everything, which had gained so much ground and was producing such important consequences in these times. The more this assertion is examined, the more true it will be found. Bentham has been in this age and country the great questioner of things established. It is by the influence of the modes of thought with which his writings inoculated a considerable number of thinking men, that the yoke of authority has been broken, and innumerable opinions, formerly received on tradition as incontestable, are put upon their defence, and required to give an account of themselves.

No one of any general information is going to accept that contention as it stands. The sceptical, questioning method of Bentham, as Mill acknowledges elsewhere, is as old and as respectable as the Platonic Socrates. The first book of *The Republic* is a clear instance of the manner in which Socrates proceeds to call into question all that has been accepted on tradition; the great value of the Socratic method being that it forces men to realize the extent to which they have remained content with empty phrases. Socrates, we remember, was put to death for corrupting the youth, an occupation Bentham practised with impunity. But we do not have to go so far back to meet with men who call into question not simply the traditions of the past (as did Hobbes and Descartes) but who call into question the very basis of those traditions such as we find them in the modern world – there are Paine and Godwin, of course, and there is also David Hume, the friend of Rousseau and Adam Smith.

Whilst Plato may properly be considered a respectable critic of traditional modes of thinking, Hume's criticism frequently rests upon explicit attitudes which step outside the pale of respectability, as here in his essay on commerce:

> It will not, I hope, be considered as a superfluous digression if I here observe, that as the multitude of mechanical arts is advantageous, so is the great number of persons to whose share the production of these arts fall. A too great disproportion among the citizens weakens any state. Every person, if possible, ought to enjoy the fruits of his labour, in a

full possession of all the necessaries, and many of the conveniences of life. No one can doubt but such an equality is most suitable to human nature, and diminishes much less from the *happiness* of the rich, than it adds to that of the poor . . .

Add to this, that were the riches are in few hands, these must enjoy all the power, and will readily conspire to lay the whole burden on the poor, and oppress them still further, to the discouragement of all industry.

On the eve of the eighteenth-century enclosures and consequent mass-unemployment, homelessness and poverty, analogous to that of the early sixteenth century, such opinions echo those of the first book of More's *Utopia* and have a similar power and unwitting revolutionary implication. What is noteworthy about Bentham's questioning, and about his method, is that it steers a middle course between the respectability of the Platonic Socrates and the anti-bourgeois humanity of Hume. And it is this which comprises its great significance for the new men of Mill's generation.

I will return to this matter later. My present point is that the significance of Bentham to those men cannot simply be accounted for in terms of the history of ideas. To say that they were influenced by Bentham does not explain why they were sympathetic to such an influence: it was not because Bentham was a sceptic and challenger of things established – so was Thomas Paine and so was William Godwin. No, what one has to consider is why the particular mode of thought which is expressed in Bentham recommended itself to men of the condition of nineteenth-century radicals. To what condition of thinking men and women does Benthamism in fact recommend itself? That is the question and it is one to which the answer may best be indicated by considering the modes of thinking of Bentham.

It may be thought unnecessary to point out that Bentham thinks and writes as a property-owning bourgeois, tending to equate the general good with the good of this class of persons. Let me, therefore, quote Mill, commending Bentham because

it is selfish interest in the form of class interest, and the class morality founded thereon, which Bentham has illustrated: the manner in which any set of persons who mix much together, and have a common interest, are apt to make that common interest their standard of virtue . . .

And it is my contention, one I shall shortly support, that Bentham himself represents such an interest and that Mill's commendations of Bentham, overlooking this, reflect the fact that Mill and Bentham share such a similar common interest; their mutual standard of virtue is thoroughly bourgeois.

> Bentham's view of the world, [as Mill points out] is that of a collection of persons pursuing each his separate interest or pleasure, and the prevention of whom from jostling one another more than is unavoidable, may be attempted by hopes and fears derived from three sources – the law, religion, and public opinion.

This became the metaphysic of the Manchester School and *laissez-faire*; it is accredited to Bentham only because it was politically expedient to turn a blind eye to its prophet, Thomas Hobbes. Keynes (a member of the Bloomsbury group for which Leavis has such a low regard) remarked that with the coming of *laissez-faire* 'the political philosopher could retire in favour of the business man – for the latter could attain the philosopher's *summum bonum* by just pursuing his own private profit'. That complacency would have been profoundly disturbed by a recollection of Hobbes's description of the state of each against all, of 'free individual competition'. Hobbes would have been horrified, no doubt, had he realized that his primitive, uncivilized 'state of nature' was not an image of the distant past but a prophetic vision of the not too distant future.

Bentham adopts the Hobbesian view of the world and all that he does, according to Mill, is 'to indicate means by which, in any given state of the national mind, the material interests of society can be protected'. He treats of the *petite morale* 'with the most pedantic minuteness' and 'on the *quid pro quo* principles which regulate trade'. Mill repeatedly refers to Benthamism as a 'means of organizing and regulating the merely *business* part of the social arrangements'. 'Business' is a term to which Mill constantly returns in describing Benthamism; he uses it ambiguously, but as a critique of Benthamism it has a specifically bourgeois connotation – it supports that characterization of Benthamite principles as similar to those 'which regulate trade'.

It is a sign of Mill's own limitations that he tends to divorce the significance of Benthamism from the spread of *laissez-faire* capitalism. To men who accepted the viewpoint of this stage of capitalist development the regulation of business had to proceed from the premise that the world was 'a collection of persons pursuing each his separate interest or pleasure' and that it was the job of the law to facilitate this individualism by reducing control to the minimum needed to prevent people from 'jostling one another more than is avoidable'. This was the principle most forcefully stated by Adam Smith, that

The natural effort of every individual to better his own condition, when suffered to exert itself with freedom and security, is so powerful a principle, that it is alone, and without an assistance, not only capable of carrying on the society to wealth and prosperity, but of surmounting a hundred impertinent obstructions with which the folly of human laws too often encumbers its operations; though the effect of these obstructions is always more or less either to encroach upon its freedom, or to diminish its security.

In brief, the outlook of *laissez-faire* capitalism chimes with that of Bentham and, as Keynes observes, 'individualism and *laissez-faire* could not, in spite of their deep roots in the political and moral philosophies of the late eighteenth and early nineteenth centuries, have secured their lasting hold over the conduct of public affairs, if it had not been for their conformity with the needs and wishes of the business world of the day'.

The connection between Benthamism and 'the needs and wishes of the business world of the day' has often been remarked. That Bentham's reform of the law would be such as to accommodate legal practice to the conditions of nineteenth-century capitalism is inadvertently illustrated by Mill when he writes that

The basis of the English law was, and still is, the feudal system. That system, like all those which existed as custom before they were established as law, possessed a certain degree of suitableness to the wants of the society among whom it grew up – that is to say, of a tribe of rude soldiers, holding a conquered people in subjection, and dividing its spoils among themselves. Advancing civilization had, however, converted this armed encampment of barbarous warriors in the midst of enemies reduced to slavery, into an industrious, commercial, rich, and free people. The laws which were suitable to the first of these states of society, could have no manner of relation to the circumstances of the second . . .

Mill is being fatuous. In the nineteenth century the robber barons still lived in an armed encampment (a truth evident to Carlyle and Arnold) and in defence of their spoils employed their soldiery against a subject people they had reduced to wage-slavery. It is symptomatic of Mill's class insularity that he should be concerned only with accommodating the law to the robber barons, who were 'industrious, commercial, rich, and free', and ignore the enslaved and impoverished masses. That kind of accommodation for the new barons is precisely what Bentham offered. Bentham's contribution to the reform of English law aimed at converting a feudal arrangement into one more in keeping with the needs of English capitalism: he wanted the law translated from the language of an old ruling class into that of a new one. And neither Bentham nor Mill show any signs of appreciating the gross inhumanity which he was thereby serving. It is true that here and there in his writings Mill criticizes the industrial-commercial society of his time, but all that he sees is a need to patch up; the socialism which he professes (as Shaw remarked) is Utilitarian socialism, what today we would call 'social democracy'.

I put the matter rather starkly in order to emphasize this second limitation, one which is due to too close an equation between what is humanly proper and what was thought to be proper by those who sought to free nineteenth-century capitalism from the trammels of the eighteenth century – for what was the anti-corn law movement, *laissez-faire*, the campaign for electoral reform, but a concerted effort to liberate the newly strengthened industrial-commercial society from the aristocratic, land-owning clutches of the eighteenth century? Bentham provided an adequate conceptual framework for such reformers; he rationalized the spirit of capitalism and reduced human happiness to a matter of computation, to be worked out on the principles of a profit and loss account.

The real strength of Bentham, then, is not to be understood by referring it to his place in the history of ideas. The history of ideas is itself nothing more than the history of more or less intelligent men confronting various problems at particular points in time and trying, as best they can, to resolve them. Bentham's real strength is that he rationalizes capitalist individualism; through Bentham the conflict between radical and conservative became reasonable. It is this very reasonableness that is to be remarked in Mill. The reasonableness of Mill, however, is quite different from the rationality of Bentham. Bentham is tough-minded and narrow-minded; he plays the Laertes to Mill's Hamlet – with this important qualification, that Bentham never allows passion to swamp cold calculation: he sets forth the ends a society ought to pursue and then demonstrates the means necessitated almost as an exercise in logic. Of course, Mill, more tender- and broad-minded than Bentham, protests that too much is sacrificed in this procedure; he wants to have the omelette without breaking the eggs. To some extent one's sympathies must go to Bentham: consider, for instance, Mill's subscription to the conservative case as put forward by Coleridge, and compare it with the Benthamite attitude.

It appears reasonable to accept, as did Coleridge – and Mill – that because men have believed something for generations there must for them have been some truth in it. But the Benthamite would certainly spot the trick here; the verbal similarity would not blind his pedantic eye to the enormous difference between *for them* and 'to them'. His response, therefore, would be that the fact that men believed something for generations only implies that they *thought* there was some truth in it; it does not imply that there *was* some truth in it. And in any case, one can imagine him adding, it is not a question of whether there was or was not some truth in it, but whether there *is* some truth in it. Furthermore, our Benthamite no doubt would continue, men believed for generations what we now know to have been complete nonsense – as, for instance, that the sun moves round a stationary flat earth. This kind of 'no nonsense' attitude must stand to the credit of Bentham. At times, as in the instance mentioned, Mill, ruffled by the bloody-mindedness of Bentham's common sense, seems to embrace Coleridge's idiocies in the mistaken belief that they shelter him from Gradgrindery.

Bentham, because he is narrow-minded and calculating, does not allow (perhaps cannot allow) his mind to become clouded by the range of emotion that often affects Mill. In some ways this limits the value of what he has to say, but in others it is a positive strength, for Bentham is immune to such things as nostalgia and sentimentality in all its forms, as plainly enough neither Mill nor Coleridge are. Thus to the Coleridge–Mill contention that because generations of men have believed something or another there must have been some truth in it, the Benthamite retort is simply that men have believed all sorts of things, some true and some false, and that the true should be kept and the false rejected. In other words, the past should receive no preferential treatment.

There is another respect in which Bentham is distinguished from Mill. Bentham is not a gentleman; the nature of his thinking is as much due to this as it is to his businessman's traits: his criticisms and conclusions are never softened by politeness. In contrast, Mill is liberally minded, that is to say that he will carefully pay his respects to the other fellow's point of view. It is not often made clear whether this is commendable on intellectual grounds as well as on grounds of good manners. Certainly that gentlemen should behave in such a manner is a rule of the Club – but that is beside the point. Coleridge adopts a similar attitude towards the past, as has been remarked earlier. It does seem to be the case that many people believe that good manners are somehow especially conducive to the discovery of truth. On reading Mill one is aware that he is giving sympathetic attention to Coleridge out of some such impulse – or, at least, that this impulse enters into Mill's considerations in an important way. It is not wrong to give such attention to Coleridge, but it is wrong to confuse the impulse to behave politely with that which inspires one to reach the truth. And because Mill seems so comfortably at home in this confusion one is ultimately aware, in reading him, of breeding rather than intelligence. This touches upon the core of the predicament which Mill is attempting to resolve in the essays on Bentham and Coleridge.

Whilst Mill finds Bentham's rationality irresistible, he is aware that Bentham lacks the finer accomplishments of a gentleman; he has no appreciation of the arts, no sense of tradition and no refinement of sentiment. The Benthamite, therefore, must go to Coleridge as a callow young lady to a finishing school – to rub the uncomfortable edges off his intellect. The conjunction of rationality of mind and cultivation of feeling surreptitiously reinstates the eighteenth-century ideal and takes the edge off Bentham. This is evident in Mill's style and colours the reader's mind. What, in reading Mill, is one's awareness of him if not an awareness of the actual character of his writing, his style? All the talk of 'mind' in which Leavis indulges surely comes down to a matter of this kind – that the character of Mill's writing reveals, or rather realizes, certain attitudes and dispositions, certain ways of coming to grips with the world, or not coming to grips with it. Let us, then turn to a paragraph, which has been selected because it represents Mill's style at its best, hence at its clearest, and is consequently symptomatic of those attitudes and dispositions which Leavis refers to as 'mind'.

A place, therefore, must be assigned to Bentham among the masters of wisdom, the great teachers and permanent intellectual ornaments of the human race. He is among those who have enriched mankind with imperishable gifts; although these do not transcend all other gifts, nor entitle him to those honours 'above all Greek, above all Roman fame', which by a natural reaction against the neglect and contempt of the world, many of his admirers were once disposed to accumulate upon him, yet to refuse an admiring recognition of what he was, on account of what he was not, is a much worse error, and one which, pardonable in the vulgar, is no longer permitted to any cultivated and instructed mind.

The style is Johnson's; it not only employs the Johnsonian vocabulary and syntax but it catches perfectly Johnson's manner of savouring language like a verbal gourmet, e.g. 'and one which, pardonable in the vulgar, is no longer permitted to any cultivated and instructed mind'. Such formulations provide an oral satisfaction which renders truth irrelevant. It expresses a state of mind which is abstracted from objective reality and seeks its pleasures in expression rather than observation. The impression of a measured and balanced judgement is an illusion created by verbal arrangement, by circumlocution and antithesis. The style is no mere affectation of the past, however; its procedures and ends realize the intention to make Bentham a more comfortable influence by accommodating Benthamism to the 'reasonableness' and cultivation of a past age: it embraces that gulf between the vulgar and the cultivated with a truly Johnsonian conservatism.

The Johnsonese is also evident when Mill turns to pronounce upon Bentham's imagination – a term which establishes other connections in the mind of the reader, as it does in that of Mill.

With Imagination in the popular sense, command of imagery and metaphorical expression, Bentham was, to a certain degree, endowed. For want, indeed of poetical culture, the images with which his fancy supplies him were seldom beautiful, but they were quaint and humorous, or bold, forcible, and intense: passages might be quoted from him both of playful irony, and of declamatory eloquence, seldom surpassed in the writings of philosophers. The Imagination which he had not, was that to which the name is generally appropriated by the best writers of the present day; that which enables us, by a voluntary effort, to conceive of the absent as if it were present, the imaginary as if it were real, and to clothe it in the feelings which, if it were indeed real, it would bring along with it. This is the power by which one human being enters into the mind and circumstances of another. This power constitutes the poet, in so far as he does anything but melodiously utter his own actual feelings.

As we read this passage we become aware of Wordsworth, a bigger figure than Johnson and Coleridge, and that Mill's feeling for the past is, in fact, a confused response not only to eighteenth-century politeness but also to the achievement of Wordsworth. It is true that the doctrine of the Imagination offered here as a standard by which to judge Bentham is expounded by Coleridge in *Biographia Literaria*, but Coleridge appears to have adopted this from Wordsworth and it is impressive because of Wordsworth's achievement, not because of Coleridge's formulation. Mill goes on to speak of Bentham's limitations in such a manner that it is impossible to avoid the realization that Bentham is being judged and found wanting in a mind profoundly influenced by Wordsworth. Thus we are told that Bentham 'had never been made alive to the unseen influences which were acting on himself, nor consequently on his fellow creatures'. And again we are told of Bentham that

Knowing so little of human feelings; he knew still less of the influences by which those feelings are formed: all the more subtle workings both of the mind upon itself, and of external things upon the mind, escaped him; and no one, probably, who, in a highly instructed age, ever attempted to give a rule to all human conduct, set out with a more limited conception either of the agencies by which human conduct *is*, or of those by which it *should* be, influenced.

In short, the standard from which Bentham falls short is that set by *The Prelude*. And the limitations remarked by Mill are limitations that have a special place in Mill's own development; limitations that were first exposed to his view, or so it would appear, by Wordsworth.

It may be that Mill was saved from the Gradgrindery of many of Bentham's admirers by the influence of Wordsworth; he himself reports the dramatic effect Wordsworth's poetry had upon him as a young man in his *Autobiography*. The effect, however, was various: it awakened him to the need for 'poetical culture', a philistine phrase which places poetry on a par with deportment; it provided him, however, with more data than Bentham and made him more acutely aware of the distinction between the quantity and quality of experience; but, finally, in bringing consideration to bear upon 'all the more subtle workings both of the mind upon itself, and of external things upon the mind', it concentrated his attention upon the mind as an ego. In this reduction of man, the effect of Wordsworth upon Mill was a denial of Wordsworth's real achievement and a local illustration of the manner in which

Wordsworth was accommodated to the psychology of *laissez-faire* liberalism. That is simply another way of saying that to understand the virtues which recommended Wordsworth (and also Bentham and Coleridge) to Mill it is necessary to recognize the 'common interest' or 'class interest' upon which his 'standard of virtue' is founded. The rest is politics.

Fantasy and Reality in
Middlemarch

George Eliot's genius has been generally agreed to lie 'in a profound analysis of the individual'. Quentin Anderson has pointed out that the novel's character analyses have been continuously referred to by critics of *Middlemarch* from George Eliot's day down to the present.

'It is notable,' Anderson has written, 'that analytic passages . . . predominate among those chosen for quotation from Leslie Stephen's day to our own. The description of Caleb Garth, of Rosamond Vincy's terrible self-absorption, of Dorothea's aspirations and her blindness to her sister Celia's world, of Bulstrode's casuistical inner life, of Casaubon's tortured consciousness of inadequacy – all these are analytic though all are matched by passages of dialogue in which their substance is exemplified. Certain dramatic scenes – that between Dorothea and Rosamond in particular – are also favourites, but again the most familiar passage about Rosamond seems to be that which describes her reaction to the awful, the inconceivable fact that there is another self in the world, one which Ladislaw cherishes far more than hers.'

The distinction between the passages of character analysis and the bulk of the writing in the novel raises questions concerning the relationship of George Eliot's characters to their setting. Arnold Kettle, for instance, has observed that George Eliot's 'setting' is seldom more than mere reportage and the justness of this observation can be judged from the following passage from the first book of *Middlemarch*:

Old provincial society had its share of subtle movement: had not only its striking downfalls, its brilliant young professional dandies who ended by living up an entry with a drab and six children for their establishment, but also those less marked vicissitudes which are constantly shifting the boundaries of social intercourse, and begetting new consciousness of interdependence. Some slipped a little downward, some got higher footing: people denied aspirates, gained wealth, and fastidious gentlemen stood for boroughs; some were caught in political currents, some in ecclesiastical, and perhaps found themselves surprisingly grouped in consequence; while a few personages or families that stood with rocky firmness amidst all this fluctuation, were slowly presenting new aspects in spite of solidity, and altering with the double change of self and beholder. Municipal and rural parish gradually made fresh threads of connections – gradually, as the old stocking gave way to the savings-bank, and worship of the solar guinea became extinct; while squires and baronets, and even lords who had once lived blamelessly afar from the civic mind, gathered the faultiness of closer acquaintanceship. Settlers, too, came from distant counties, some with an alarming novelty of skill, others with an offensive advantage in cunning. In fact, much the same sort of movement and mixture went on in old England as we find in older Herodotus, who also, in telling what had been, thought it well to take a woman's lot for his starting point . . .

We have, then, a distinction between the high order of George Eliot's prose when creating character in analysis and the competent, workmanlike prose in which the social milieu is placed before us. Consequently, some critics (including Kettle and Anderson) have remarked upon the important distinction thereby drawn by George Eliot between individual character and social milieu. Kettle sees the discrepancy in the prose of *Middlemarch* abstractly, as a discrepancy between lively individuals and a static society and then proceeds to criticize George Eliot for her mechanistic account of the relationship between the individual and society. In this Kettle is mistaken on a number of counts. For instance, in the passage on 'old provincial society' quoted above, society is not conceived as static but as fluctuating and the liveliness of individuals, the rising and falling and shifting of positions, is seen in terms of this fluctuation. Furthermore, the social types mentioned in the passage are not dissociated from the characters we meet with in the novel: 'Settlers, too, came from distant counties, some with an alarming novelty of skill [Lydgate], others with an offensive advantage in cunning [Bulstrode].' Indeed, I think it will be found that the types mentioned in the passage are all realized in the characterization of the novel. That society in Middlemarch is static in the sense that it is not seen to be developing, which may be what Kettle has in mind, is not true either: money is replacing gentility, Brooke is embracing the Whig party – surely important developments in old provincial society. It hardly needs to be said that such a society does not accept change willingly, as witness the reception of Lydgate's notions on medical reform or those of Dorothea concerning the improvement of cottages, or of Brooke and Ladislaw at election time. Reform is in the air, but it is defeated; Lydgate is defeated, so are Ladislaw, Brooke and Dorothea. From this it is to be concluded not that society is static but that old provincial society is still tough in Middlemarch, as it was in most such places at the beginning of the nineteenth century.

It seems to me that Kettle is not criticizing George Eliot but the society she depicts so well. As for George Eliot's attitude to that society, I don't think she could be said to approve of it. The most that can be said about this whole matter is that Middlemarch represents, for all its multiplicity and fluctuation, an essentially conservative mode of life, allergic to change but not impervious or unmoved and unaffected by it. In the novel iself there is a distinction between individual hopes and aspirations and a tough, down-to-earth provincial scepticism and common sense, such as we find in Celia's attitude towards her high-flown sister. It may be the presence of this stubborn, sceptical conservatism that led Kettle to believe that,

> because the Middlemarch world is the given, static reality, the characters of the novel must be seen as at its mercy . . ,

and Anderson to claim much the same, although in different terms:

> George Eliot has created a common medium which completely immerses most of her characters. It is hard to conceive how an individual can on this scene really originate anything.

Anderson's statement no doubt strikes the reader as provisionally true. The stubborn conservatism of provincial society is implicit in George Eliot's conception of her St. Theresa theme as this is set out in the Prelude to *Middlemarch*; it is precisely this which is seen as frustrating would-be St. Theresas, male and female, and the manner in which it does so can be seen by turning to specific passages – the hospital board meeting, the election meeting, the scene in the pub, the attack upon the railway surveyors. In such passages the forces which frustrate reform are very clearly realized.

However, it isn't merely the provincial scepticism of Middlemarch that turns aspirations into a fool's paradise; no dreams are shattered by meeting any 'given, static reality' head on. Mr. Vincy dreaming of the mayoralty, Fred Vincy dreaming of Featherstone's fortune, Lydgate dreaming of medical reform, Ladislaw and Brooke of winning over the Middlemarch voters, Dorothea of helping in some great work, Casaubon of his *Key to All Mythologies* – all these dreams or aspirations have an air of self-delusion about them and self-delusion is not restricted to the obvious aspirants of Middlemarch, it serves equally well to characterize Rosamond Vincy and Bulstrode. The dream world is defeated not because it is aspiring, but because it has no tangible connection with the solid realities of Middlemarch; it is punctured invariably by sharp, precise contact with these realities – by a will, a blackmailer, a marriage, a commercial crisis. What the dreams lack is that grip upon the world characterized in Celia; the dreamers' attitude to the world outside themselves is shamefaced, as Dorothea is shamefaced at the sinking of her hopes that the cottages at Lowick would be bad enough to require restoration and reform. In short, the dreams or aspirations are delusions simply because they have no grasp of the world of Middlemarch.

This last observation is consistent with the narrative attitude of the novel, in which, with ironic detachment and sarcasm, the lofty yearnings of the aspirants are viewed through common eyes. As the author remarks of latter-day St. Theresas in the Prelude,

with dim lights and tangled circumstance they tried to shape their thought and deed in noble agreement; but after all, to common eyes their struggles seemed mere inconsistency and formlessness . . .

The remark applies aptly to such a passage as that in which Celia refers to Dorothea's 'favourite fad to draw plans', to the sharing of the jewels between Celia and Dorothea, to Vincy's interview with Bulstrode, and to many other passages throughout the novel. These are passages in which the ironic detachment and sarcasm of the narrator are heaviest and in which we most evidently view the lofty effort through common eyes. That this is so gives rise to a most important consideration.

Let us suppose, as we are given leave to in the Prelude, that the primary concern of the novel is with those lofty yearnings which are frustrated by old provincial society. It would seem from the Prelude that the balance of favour lies with the potential St. Theresas and is tilted against the society which frustrates them. This would appear to be the bias of the final sentence of the Prelude –

> Here and there is born a St. Theresa, foundress of nothing, whose loving heart-beats and sobs after an unattained goodness tremble off and are dispersed among hindrances, instead of centering in some long-recognizable deed.

– and the whole of the Prelude tilts this way. The bias of the narrative, however, is in quite the opposite direction, favours the viewpoint, the scepticism of the common eye, the eye of old provincial society.

The novel, then, is a critical inspection of the Prelude's St. Theresa thesis. In the course of this inspection it does not place the lofty reforms and tasks that have captured the imaginations of Lydgate, Dorothea, Bulstrode, Ladislaw and Brooke as utopian, but reveals the incapacity of these characters to realize their dreams. In short, the illusions from which these and other characters suffer are illusions about themselves. Consequently, Anderson's remark, that 'It is hard to conceive how an individual can on this scene really originate anything', needs to be corrected by observing that the failure to really originate anything is not due to the scene but to the individual character; as a supreme instance of this consider Casaubon and his *Key to All Mythologies*. Similarly, Dorothea and the unregenerate Fred Vincy are both 'disposed rather to accuse the intolerable narrowness and the purblind conscience of . . . society' than to admit any error in themselves. The point is made by the narrator following the altercation between Celia and Dorothea on the subject of Dorothea's schemes:

> Celia could not help relenting. 'Poor Dodo,' she went on, in an amiable staccato. 'It is very hard: it is your favourite *fad* to draw plans.'
> '*Fad* to draw plans! Do you think I only care about my fellow-creatures' houses in that childish way? I may well make mistakes. How can one ever do anything nobly Christian, living among people with such petty thoughts?'
> No more was said: Dorothea was too much jarred to recover her temper and behave so as to show that she admitted any error in herself. She was disposed rather to accuse the intolerable narrowness and the purblind conscience of the society around her . . .

Dorothea's lament is so similar to Anderson's comment upon the novel as a whole that the narrator's observation may be allowed to extend to it. Anderson is rather too disposed to accuse the 'scene' for the characters' failure to originate anything.

On reading the novel one very soon comes to realize that the lofty characters are remarkable similar, even in their loftiest moments, to the mundane and purblind ones. Rosamond in contemplating her marriage can achieve a state of day-dream as far removed from actuality as any which Dorothea entertains when contemplating hers. Having only just met Lydgate, Rosamond rides home with her brother:

> Rosamond, whose basis for her structure had the usual airy slightness, was of remarkable detailed and realistic imagination when the foundation had been once presupposed; and before they had ridden a mile she was far on in the costume and introductions of her wedded life, having determined on her house in Middlemarch, and foreseen the visits she would pay to her husband's high-bred relatives at a distance, whose finished manners she could appropriate as thoroughly as she had done her school accomplishments, preparing herself thus for vaguer elevations which might ultimately come.

Rosamond here is very much like Dorothea; the passage could well be a parody of Dorothea's day-dreams and speculations, even down to Rosamond's desire to appropriate finished manners thus preparing herself 'for vaguer elevations which might ultimately come', which parodies Dorothea's desire to appropriate some of Casaubon's knowledge and so prepare herself 'for vaguer elevations'.

It is this perception of the basic similarity of the worldly and the most unworldly that accounts for the common-eye viewpoint of the narrative: basically Dorothea is of the same stuff as Rosamond and by bringing them within the same focus the common-eye view expresses this realization. How it does so can be seen from the passage on the sharing of the jewels and, at greater length, in the following passage.

> It had not entered Dorothea's mind that Mr Casaubon might wish to make her his wife, and the idea that he would do so touched her with a sort of reverential gratitude. How good of him – nay, it would be almost as if a winged messenger had suddenly stood beside her path and held out his hand towards her! For a long while she had been

oppressed by the indefiniteness which hung in her mind, like a thick summer haze, over all her desire to make her life greatly effective. What could she do, what ought she to do? – she, hardly more than a budding woman, but yet with an active conscience and a great mental need, not to be satisfied by a girlish instruction comparable to the nibblings and judgements of a discursive mouse. With some endowment of stupidity and conceit, she might have thought that a Christian young lady of fortune should find her ideal of life in village charities, patronage of the humbler clergy, the perusal of 'Female Scripture Characters', unfolding the private experience of Sara under the Old Dispensation, and Dorcas under the New, and the care of her soul over her embroidery in her own boudoir – with a background of prospective marriage to a man who, if less strict than herself, as being involved in affairs religiously inexplicable, might be prayed for and seasonably exhorted. From such contentment poor Dorothea was shut out. The intensity of her religious disposition, the coercion it exercised over her life, was but one aspect of a nature altogether ardent, theoretic, and intellectually consequent: and with such a nature, struggling in the bands of a narrow teaching, hemmed in by a social life which seemed nothing but a labyrinth of petty courses, a walled-in maze of small paths that led no whither, the outcome was sure to strike others as at once exaggeration and inconsistency. The thing which seemed to her best, she wanted to justify by the completest knowledge; and not to live in a pretended admission of rules which were never acted on. Into this soul-hunger as yet all her youthful passion was poured; the union which attracted her was one that would deliver her from her girlish subjection to her own ignorance, and give her the freedom of voluntary submission to a guide who would take her along the grandest path.

'I should learn everything then,' she said to herself, still walking quickly along the bridle road through the wood. 'It would be my duty to study that I might help him the better in his great works. There would be nothing trivial about our lives. Everyday-things with us would mean the greatest things. It would be like marrying Pascal. I should learn to see the truth by the same light as great men have seen it by. And then I should know what to do, when I got older; I should see how it was possible to lead a grand life here – now – in England. I don't feel sure about doing good in any way now: everything seems like going on a mission to a people whose language I don't know; – unless it were building good cottages – there can be no doubt about that. Oh, I hope I should be able to get the people well housed in Lowick! I will draw plenty of plans while I have time.'

Dorothea checked herself suddenly with self-rebuke for the presumptuous way in which she was reckoning on uncertain events, but she was spared any inward effort to change the direction of her thoughts by the appearance of a cantering horseman round a turning of the road. The well-groomed chestnut horse and two beautiful setters could leave no doubt that the rider was Sir James Chettam. He discerned Dorothea, jumped off his horse at once, and, having delivered it to his groom, advanced towards her with something white on his arm, at which the two setters were barking in an excited manner.

'How delightful to meet you, Miss Brooke,' he said, raising his hat and showing his sleekly-waving blond hair. 'It has hastened the pleasure I was looking forward to.'

Miss Brooke was annoyed at the interruption. This amiable baronet, really a suitable husband for Celia, exaggerated the necessity of making himself agreeable to the elder sister. Even a prospective brother-in-law may be an oppression if he will always be presupposing too good an understanding with you, and agreeing with you even when you contradict him. The thought that he had made the mistake of paying his addresses to herself could not take shape: all her mental activity was used up in persuasions of another kind. But he was positively obtrusive at his moment, and his dimpled hands were quite disagreeable. Her roused temper made her colour deeply, as she returned his greeting with some haughtiness.

Sir James interpreted the heightened colour in the way most gratifying to himself, and thought he never saw Miss Brooke looking so handsome.

'I have brought a little petitioner,' he said, 'or rather, I have brought him to see if he will be approved before his petition is offered.' He showed the white object under his arm, which was a tiny Maltese puppy, one of nature's most naïve toys.

'It is painful to me to see these creatures that are bred merely as pets,' said Dorothea, whose opinion was forming itself that very moment (as opinions will) under the heat of irritation.

'Oh, why?' said Sir James, as they walked forward.

'I believe all the petting that is given them does not make them happy. They are too helpless: their lives are too frail. A weasel or a mouse that gets its own living is more interesting. I like to think that the animals about us have souls something like our own, and either carry on their own little affairs or can be companions to us, like Monk here. Those creatures are parasitic.'

'I am so glad I know that you do not like them,' said good Sir James. 'I should never keep them for myself, but ladies usually are fond of these Maltese dogs. Here, John, take this dog, will you?'

The objectionable puppy, whose nose and eyes were equally black and expressive, was thus got rid of, since Miss Brooke decided that it had better not have been born. But she felt it necessary to explain.

'You must not judge of Celia's feeling from mine. I think she likes these small pets. She had a tiny terrier once, which she was very fond of. It made me unhappy, because I was afraid of treading on it. I am rather short-sighted.'

'You have your own opinion about everything, Miss Brooke, and it is always a good opinion.'

What answer was possible to such stupid complimenting?

'Do you know, I envy you that,' Sir James said, as they continued walking at the rather brisk pace set by Dorothea.

'I don't quite understand what you mean.'

'Your power of forming an opinion. I can form an opinion of persons. I know when I like people. But about other matters, do you know, I have often a difficulty in deciding. One hears very sensible things said on opposite sides.'

'Or that seem sensible. Perhaps we don't always discriminate between sense and nonsense.'

Dorothea felt that she was rather rude.

'Exactly,' said Sir James. 'But you seem to have the power of discrimination.'

'On the contrary, I am often unable to decide. But that is from ignorance. The right conclusion is there all the same, though I am unable to see it.'

'I think there are few who would see it more readily. Do you know, Lovegood was telling me yesterday that you had the best notion in the world of a plan for cottages – quite wonderful for a young lady, he thought. You had a real *genus*, to use his expression. He said you wanted Mr. Brooke to build a new set of cottages, but he seemed to think it hardly probable that your uncle would consent. Do you know, that is one of the things I wish to do – I mean, on my own estate. I should be so glad to carry out that plan of yours, if you would let me see it. Of course, it is sinking money; that is why people object to it.

Labourers can never pay rent to make it answer. But, after all, it is
worth doing.'

'Worth doing! yes, indeed,' said Dorothea, energetically,
forgetting her previous small vexations. 'I think we deserve to be
beaten out of our beautiful houses with a scourge of small cords – all of
us who let tenants live in such sties as we see round us. Life in cottages
might be happier than ours, if they were real houses fit for human
beings from whom we expect duties and affections.'

'Will you show me your plan?'

'Yes, certainly. I daresay it is very faulty. But I have been examining
all the plans for cottages in Loudon's book, and picked out what seem
the best things. Oh what a happiness it would be to set the pattern
about here! I think, instead of Lazarus at the gate, we should put the
pig-sty cottages outside the park-gate.'

Dorothea was in the best temper now. Sir James, as brother-in-law,
building model cottages on his estate, and then, perhaps, others being
built at Lowick, and more and more elsewhere in imitation – it would
be as if the spirit of Oberlin had passed over the parishes to make the
life of poverty beautiful!

There is much that could be said about this lengthy passage, about the
ironic force of the opening – 'How good of him' – the comic view of the
normal plight of females – 'a background of prospective marriage to a
man who, if less strict than herself, as being involved in affairs religiously
inexplicable, might be prayed for and seasonably exhorted' – the touch
of humorous pathos in 'poor Dorothea', the comic immaturity of
Dorothea's 'I will draw plenty of plans while I have time'. Consider also
Dorothea, 'whose opinion was forming itself that very moment' being
complimented, with unconscious humour, by Sir James on her 'power of
forming an opinion'. There is a similar ironic humour in Dorothea's
confession, 'I am rather short-sighted', especially as addressed to Sir
James, whom she purblindly believes to be enamoured of her sister. But
what requires particular attention in the passage is the rapidly changing
mood and temper of Dorothea. She is touched to begin with 'with a sort
of reverential gratitude', checks her fancies with 'self-rebuke', is
immediately 'annoyed at the interruption' of Sir James's appearance –
'he was positively obtrusive . . . and his dimpled hands were quite
disagreeable. Her roused temper made her colour deeply. . . .'
Eventually Sir James turns to her projects for cottages and Dorothea at
once forgets her vexations, 'Dorothea was in the best temper now.'

Dorothea is a mercurial character, subject to rapid and numerous changes of mood and temper. In this (whatever one's view of the stereotype may be) she is presented as essentially feminine in temperament; she is far more feminine and volatile than Rosamond Vincy. She is, as Celia truly observes in the jewels episode, inconsistent; she is extravagant and impulsive, as Celia also observes, following the incidents described in the passage quoted at length above, and Celia has to point out to her that people are staring, not listening. Dorothea, then, is impulsive, inconsistent and mercurial.

This brings me back to the preoccupation of *Middlemarch* with the vague, fantastic, dream stuff and the down-to-earth, the specific and the concrete. This preoccupation shapes the character of Dorothea; she is not simply a creature of the dream-world, given over to her own private fantasies. Over and against her fantasies is set her vitality and ebullience. The character has a vital, shifting relationship with everything that comes into contact with it. However, these fluctuations of regard and disposition are very much of a piece with those more pervasive fluctuations which characterize 'old provincial society'. What we observe in the characterization of Dorothea is the nature of George Eliot's insight: what we have is a shifting, impulsive and inconsistent world, a world of folly, ignorance, enthusiasm, day-dream and scepticism, all compounding together in ever-changing portions. It is a world to which the volatile Dorothea belongs, in the sense that she expresses that same compound and unstable mixture, just as Bulstrode, Lydgate and Rosamund also belong, although none of these express the nature of the novel's world as well as Dorothea.

The substantial point is that there is no fundamental distinction between Middlemarch society, the world or social milieu of the novel, and the individual characters so profoundly analysed. The close analytic attention paid to the characters instances the novel's critical inspection of the St. Theresa thesis that old provincial society frustrated those who desired to perform great and noble deeds. If the tenor of the inspection is dispiriting, it is so because it communicates an historical truth which Mill ignores: there are definite, social conditions under which ideas and ideals become a material force in the world. And it is in consequence of its recognition of this truth that *Middlemarch*, which begins in the realm of personal idealism and private fantasy, ends in the realm of politics.

Index